Who Among Giants

Principles and Profiles in Service for an Arriving Generation

Peter Gariepy

This is a work of non-fiction. Except for use in reviews, please do not copy or reproduce the text of this book without permission. For permissions, inquiries regarding appearances or bulk purchases, or other questions, please contact the author at contact@gariepy.org, or via Twitter at @GariePeter.

Cover design by Emir Orucevic of pulpstudio, via 99designs.com. Back cover photograph and photograph of the author on page 165 by Two Lillies Photography.

Library of Congress Cataloging in Publication Data:

Gariepy, Peter (1983-),
ong Giants: Principles and Profiles in Service for an Arriving Generation.
ISBN 978-0-692-05574-8
1. Gariepy, Peter (1983-) 2. United States—Politics and Government—21st Century. 3. United States—Politics and Government—Local Government.
4. Chicago (IL)—History. 5. Chicago (IL)—Biography.

328.7309 GAR

V. 1.0

To Karishma, forever the best part of my life.

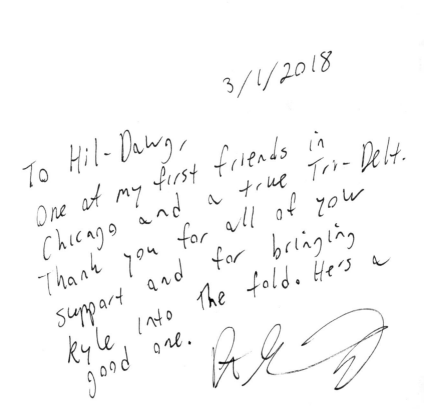

3/1/2018

To Hil-Dawg,
One of my first friends in Tri-Delt.
Chicago and a true Tri-Delt.
Thank you for all of your
support and for bringing
kyle into the fold. He's a
good one.

Contents

A Note to the Reader

Himself an elected official, Thomas Jefferson once said, "[t]he most valuable of all talents is that of never using two words when one will do." Most, if not all, candidates and elected officials are impelled to keep talking well beyond the point of what's sufficient. Maybe it's ego that drives a person to ask for the faith and support of voters they may never meet, or for regular reassurance that their ideas are compelling, or for confirmation that their personality is appealing. Likely guilty of all three, I hope that writing in a spirit of honesty and self-awareness will keep this book concise and enjoyable out of respect for the reader's generous gift of time.

Who Among Giants

Principles and Profiles in Service for an Arriving Generation

Chapter 1

Who Among Giants

I n the leap from concern to candidacy, a citizen once elected risks becoming a politician. Maybe a politician is born out of political ambition that, consciously or subconsciously, influences his behavior, perspective, and long- and short-term goals. Maybe a politician exists the moment the vote is certified and a candidate wins his first election, whether for the White House or the local school council. Perhaps a politician is simply any elected official who believes himself equal to or greater than the office in which he temporarily serves at the pleasure of the voters.

Either way, the word "politician" has become a pejorative the public can use to vilify its elected leaders in an attempt to keep them in check. Hilariously, some candidates, including incumbents who are, perhaps, politicians *themselves, try to appear aligned with public frustration by criticizing those very politicians whose ranks they are campaigning to join or remain among.*

Perhaps the mark of a worthwhile elected official is a willingness to bear the scarlet letter of a politician without succumbing to the temptations of greed and laziness as did their predecessors who tarnished the word. Perhaps it requires a willingness to put your good name on the line for the principles that tug you from your private life onto the ballot and to face the risk of being seen as (or, worse, becoming) one of the elected officials whose past judgment and behavior rightfully leads to the scrutiny of the purity of your own motives. The risk of becoming a politician should be outweighed by an individual's desire to do good—and good that can be done in no other place than the elected office being sought.

❧

As I write this, I am running for the Democratic nomination for Cook County Treasurer. Named for Illinois's first attorney general, Daniel Cook, Cook County is America's second most populous county, behind Los Angeles County, and is one of the Democratic party's historic and lasting strongholds. At the seat of Cook County sits Chicago, and at the heart of Cook County exists a political landscape that lives up to its reputation as endlessly intense and fascinating.

The point of this book is to articulate my values and to explain what drew me to engage civically and pursue public office for the first time, not as a career, but as an opportunity to improve the system for the long term even if I am part of it for only one term. My hope is that this book is, at worst, a plotless and somewhat entertaining collection of ideas and reflections and, at best, a valuable investment of your attention that leads to you taking a new step into impacting your community, your industry, or your government through increased civic engagement.

Elected officials are endowed with power to impact our lives for better and for worse. As voters, we must look at the kinds of people, such as myself, who are attracted to the current political process that must be navigated to serve in office and ask ourselves if these are the types of people we want leading our legislatures, agencies, and executive offices. If we determine that such people are not who we want as leaders, we must then investigate how our political and electoral system can and should be adjusted or reimagined to attract those who are better suited for these consequential responsibilities.

At thirty-five years old, with my wife and me having celebrated five years of marriage, our toddler daughter walking and talking up a storm, and me entering the vortex of Chicago area politics, I am learning how to advance the ideals that inspire me while working within the reality in which I must operate. It was the careful consideration of those ideals that motivated me to run that also led to this book. Of course, writing a book is not required to run for office, so why should someone just beginning to gain political experience have any business writing a book on the topic? Believe me, I asked myself that question too. Put bluntly, I believe that I owe it to voters to disclose the wide-reaching and deeply held values that drove me to ask for their vote.

I don't know if my campaign will be successful, so regardless of whether I am elected in this or any future attempts, I want to articulate the principles and the accompanying' emotions and logic and anecdotes that drove me to run before my perspective is at greater risk of becoming that of a stereotypical politician, something to which I hope never to succumb. Any constituency I am fortunate enough to serve will rightfully deserve an explanation should I violate the core principles laid out in this book, so it was an exhilarating challenge to write something that I will have to stand by in the future, while knowing that my positions will evolve with the accumulation of experience and information.

When I began writing this book, I sought to reflect the principles of pragmatism, innovation, respect, and empathy that I hope pervade my current campaign and any time in public office I am fortunate enough to receive from voters. This book is intended to be more philosophical than political, and it is for anyone thinking of taking a step toward civic engagement, which might include running for office, getting involved with neighborhood associations, or participating in a voter registration drive.

I hope this book will be a helpful lens through which others can examine their contributions to society and play larger roles in their communities in order to better advocate for their priorities.

Competition is a wonderfully revealing crucible in which you can truly learn and expand your limits. While the heat of a challenge can fuel growth and, hopefully, victory, it can be all-consuming at the expense of one's health (both physical and mental) and ever-fleeting time with family. In the year before his death at age forty-three, legendary comedian John Candy starred as a bobsled coach in search of redemption in Disney's movie *Cool Runnings*. In a scene with the impetuous leader of the Jamaican bobsled team he is guiding to an Olympic bid, Candy's character revealed that as a bobsledder himself years earlier, he was stripped of his Olympic gold medal for cheating. After admitting his disgrace, he says, "a gold medal is a wonderful thing, but if you're not enough without it, you'll never be enough with it." Adrenaline from competition must never be allowed to pollute my character, which no victory is worth. Sometimes it's not worth the win. If elected, I must be proud of how I did it, and if I lose, it has to be with no regrets.

❧

Tucked along the eastern edge of the Chicago River in the River North neighborhood stands Erie Café, a red brick steakhouse that has served Chicago for generations and has traditionally hosted another institution that spans the generations: The Democratic Party of Cook County. During the Party's biannual meeting, the Party's eighty committeemen (an elected and unpaid Democratic Party representative from each of Chicago's fifty wards and the county's thirty surrounding townships) gather to hear speeches from the candidates seeking the Party's endorsement and to vote on which candidates to include on the list or "slate" of endorsed candidates for countywide and statewide offices.

As a candidate for the Democratic nomination for Cook County Treasurer, and a first-time candidate for public office at any level, I entered Erie Café around 8:30 a.m. on Thursday, August 10, 2017, to make the case for why my candidacy should be endorsed over that of a twenty-year incumbent who had not faced a primary challenger since initially being elected. Before Erie Café opened that morning, I sat in the back of a nearby coffee shop, anxiously reviewing my prepared remarks, which, in accordance with the meeting's guidelines, had been condensed into a precisely-timed three minutes. When the time came, I walked into the sun-filled and relatively empty steakhouse, where I saw my opponent. With the same sense of shaking hands with the other team's starting lineup prior to kickoff, I walked over to say good morning and good luck. After all, my competitor need not be my enemy.

With an outstretched hand and a bit of naïveté about the reception I was about to receive, my "good morning" prompted an exchange that went something like this:

"Can I speak to you off on the side for a minute?" she asked.

"Sure," I replied.

"Why are you doing this?"

"Why am I here today or why am I running?"

"Did someone put you up to this?"

"No, I made the decision to run."

"You know when you walk in there today, you're among giants."

After the "giant" warning, which I took as a crack at intimidation, we separately made our way into the banquet room at the back of the restaurant to mingle with the growing crowd of committeemen, proxies of absent committeemen, other Democratic operatives, and a few members of the media.

As the youngest and likely least-known of the candidates, I politely introduced myself to as many people as possible in the hope that they would spend more of the three minutes of my allotted speaking time listening to my remarks rather than wondering how to pronounce my last name, which rhymes with "therapy." Was everyone in that room a giant? I certainly was not, and I was about to stand before them.

After the first few speakers made their remarks, the meeting's chairman, Alderman Roderick Sawyer of Chicago's 6th Ward, invited me to the podium, whereupon I launched into my precisely timed speech:

> Good morning, my name is Peter Gariepy, and I am running to be the Democratic nominee for Cook County Treasurer. My wife and I live in the First Ward with our one-year-old daughter and our rescue dog. I have been in contact with all eighty Committeeman since beginning this effort, am grateful to those who have expressed support for our campaign, and am deeply appreciative of the perspective I've gained from conversations with many of you.

I went on a little more about my background, offered a few initiatives I'd pursue if elected, and emphasized an important point to the elected officials and any giants who were present:

> In this room are many public servants whose contributions span multiple terms, and who have never taken their time in office, or the privilege to serve, for granted. You have my gratitude and respect for never letting your offices run on autopilot. For being available and proactive for your constituents, not just when you're up for election or you have a challenger.

Not every giant is a dinosaur. Many giants continue to earn their incumbency with every term entrusted to them by the voters. Some giants become dinosaurs when they believe they're too big to be moved and too grand to be replaced, despite spending their time lazily grazing or pursuing only smaller, easier prey. And some giants at risk of becoming dinosaurs are legacy political machines that must nimbly and continuously evolve at a rate no slower than that of the modern electorate.

I answered questions asked by a few of the committeemen, expressed my gratitude for the opportunity to speak, and exited through the back of the room as my opponent entered. During the slating meeting, it is a customary courtesy for candidates to leave the room when an opponent for the same office speaks. On my way out, I said hello to a few familiar faces running for other offices who were waiting for their turn and who I had met on the summer's circuit of candidate interview panels and meetings across Cook County, which is a big county and a small world.

Exiting Erie Café into a bright and warm August morning, I felt of a wave of confidence and belonging as I loosened my tie, started the thirty-minute walk back to my office, and pondered "Who am I to stand among, challenge, and disrupt a self-described giant." It's a rhetorical question that doesn't deserve a question mark. I am a husband and father running for public office, driven by my belief in progressive values as a member of the

Millennial generation whose time to pursue positions of leadership has indeed arrived. We are the babies of Baby Boomers. We are now adults with our own households and loved ones for whom we are responsible, and it is our time to step forward and serve in the institutions that we were born to leave better than they are today.

While not true across the board, with advances in medical care and knowledge and Americans living longer than ever before, our lives can be seen in acts of thirty years. The first thirty years are for growing up, attaining formal education, and beginning to establish oneself, professionally and socially. The next thirty years is about contributing to society and pursuing and embracing leadership in areas of personal and professional interest. I won't call the next thirty years the final act because it would be nice to live a healthy fruitful life beyond ninety years of age, but let's say the third act of any generation is the time to make sure that the positions of leadership in which one has served are thoughtfully and successfully undertaken by a deep bench of qualified and compassionate successors. Generation X assumed a junior leadership role alongside Baby Boomers as the Greatest Generation moved on, and now is the time for Millennials, also known as Generation Y, to assume that role. In turn Generation X is moving into the more senior leadership position that Baby Boomers are vacating as they proceed to their next act. A generation's third act is not synonymous with surrendering what it has built or fading into retirement, but is rather a signal to the younger generation that the time has arrived to embrace and address the issues they are inheriting, as was done by previous generations, who did their best to improve the world as it existed when they entered adulthood.

Now at the threshold of leadership and responsibility, my generation owes it to ourselves and the generations on either side of us to use every resource available, which means acting on scientific fact, empathy, and the lessons of history to advance the interest of the common good during our generation's prime, so that when the time arrives to pass the baton to the next generation we can look them in the eye not with a perfect record, but with a clear conscience.

The Quaker missionary Étienne de Grellet once said, "I shall pass this way but once; any good that I can do or any kindness I can show to any human being, let me do it now. Let me not defer nor neglect it, for I shall not pass this way again." For everyone, particularly my fellow Millennials, this is our chance, our finite and limited engagement. Now is not the time to wait for an invitation; rather, it is our time to confidently step forward and lead in accordance with principles of inclusion, innovation, and fairness, and to make decisions driven by data more than habit or custom.

The older I get, the more I appreciate a quote from the comedy classic *The Jerk*. Steve Martin's sweet but dimwitted jerk is approached by a gas station owner, played by Jackie Mason, who offers the jerk a job as an attendant by asking if he'd like to be the president of Texaco Oil. Martin's character excitedly accepts, and his new employer remarks how kids today "wanna start on the top and work their way sideways." Mason's timeless wit accurately applies to pursuing public office, where there is no blueprint to guaranteed success.

Run for Something is an organization that supports progressive Millennial candidates who are thirty-five years old or younger. When asked how a potential first-time candidate can get started, Run for Something advised, "Figure out the problem you want to solve. Find the office that lets you solve it. (It's usually something local.)"

In a December 2016 post to Apple's employee message board, CEO Tim Cook wrote that:

> With so many things that we've done, we don't do it because there's a return on investment. We don't do it because we know exactly how we're going to use it. We do it because it's clear it's interesting and it might lead somewhere. A lot of the time it doesn't, but many times it leads us somewhere where we had no idea in the beginning.

In a way, Jackie Mason, Run for Something and Tim Cook are all making the point that there is not always a clear and retraceable path to your goal. Sometimes you have to work sideways toward the impact you want to generate without knowing if the originally desired result will be achieved. But if our conscience guides our curiosity, we have far greater odds of becoming a positive force in the lives of others in ways that could not have been predicted. That is why I am running for Cook County Treasurer; to shake up an office that has not scratched the surface of its enormous potential to demonstrate how taxpayers should be treated and empowered so that, from a relationship built on greater trust and confidence between the government and its citizens, vast and bold taxpayer-funded public projects can unlock opportunities for Americans of every generation, income level, ethnic background and zip code.

In my current race, to paraphrase former Illinois congressman Abner Mikva, "I am nobody that nobody sent." I have zero name recognition. This is not a complaint; it's just reality. So, while it might appear to some that I've set my sights too high for my first campaign, my choice was intentional. There are very specific problems I want to be a part of solving, and right now, the treasurer's office is the most direct route to solving them.

∽

Anything truly worth winning must also be worth risking. Running for office asks too much of oneself and loved ones to only be a candidate who will brave a path of least resistance. For those potential candidates who languish in waiting for an invitation to run for an open seat rather than stepping forward, if an office is important enough to run for, then it also must be important enough to run for regardless of whether the incumbent is ready to abdicate. The office is always more important than the occupant, and if the office can be better served then the sub-optimal occupant must be challenged. This is the attitude that must saturate the Millennial generation's approach to the political arena. We will not win every race. But if you want to do something, take the steps to do it. Don't just make anonymous comments into the dark or share your thoughts only with like-minded people. If you are qualified to run for something and you are ready to commit to your candidacy, then go do it! Waiting on the sidelines until an incumbent is ready to surrender something they do not own usually results in the election of a handpicked successor or political appointee who's likely obligated to support the status quo. Elected officials bound to such interests will not expeditiously or aggressively draft and support policies that can liberate people from systemic and inherited obstacles that unjustly limit access to opportunity.

There are very specific problems I want to help solve and the treasurer's office is the most direct route to solving them. If fortunate enough to be elected, the best way to leave the office better than when I entered, is to make sure it is regularly attracting the most innovative and driven minds to run for it, which will only strengthen the progressive brand and raise the number of future qualified candidates.

My great-grandfather died of a heart attack in 1972, eight years before my parents ever met. Growing up, I'd occasionally hear stories of him at family events. But most of what I know about my great-grandfather, Louis Joseph Gariepy, is from his semiautobiographical book titled *Saw-Ge-Mah*. Translated from the native language of the Ottawa tribe that was indigenous to northern Michigan, with whom my great-grandfather had ties, Saw-Ge-Mah means "Medicine Man." My great-grandfather shared a similar path with his book's protagonist, Hal Adams, who hailed from a small logging town, became a pharmacist before attending medical school at the University of Michigan, settled in Detroit, started a family, and cofounded a Catholic hospital.

Dr. Louis J. Gariepy was busy with his surgical clinic in northwest Detroit, serving as chief of staff and chief of the surgical staff at Mount Carmel Mercy hospital, attending surgeon at Detroit Receiving Hospital, a Fellow of the American College of Surgeons, where he served for four years as Secretary of the International College of Surgeons, and as a husband and father of three children. Without the necessary time to write the book his great-grandson would one day read, it was not until my great-grandfather was convicted of federal tax evasion and incarcerated that he was imposed with—or granted with, depending on your point of view—the time to write the book that remains my primary connection to him.

While it is shameful that my great-grandfather broke the law, I am grateful that he embraced his sentence as an opportunity to preserve his thoughts and experiences in print. It is with a similar hope for recording the lessons and beliefs that drew me to run for public office that I am writing this book. I firmly believe that those who hold public office have an obligation to their constituents to be open about what matters to them, and this book is one more way to capture and communicate my values.

My political awakening began during then-Illinois State Senator Obama's national rise when I heard his 2004 speech to the Democratic National Convention nominating Senator John Kerry of Massachusetts as the party's presidential nominee. I remain a staunch admirer of Barack Obama the president, but also often seek guidance, especially during my current campaign, from Barack Obama the young husband who navigated fatherhood and the Chicago area's political landscape of the 1990s.

Any similarities between the president and me are at best slim and coincidental. As someone who, like Obama, also is not from a politically connected family, my decision to step into politics is entirely my own. If my current campaign is successful, I will also be thirty-five when I first serve in public office; and with a relatively young family, I never want my political ambition to endanger the sense of priority that my wife and daughter should always feel from me. It is from this angle that I look to State Senator Barack Obama for guidance, while benefiting from the hindsight of a man who would ably protect, love, and nurture his family under the most unforgiving and isolating of spotlights.

Christopher Andersen's 2009 book, *Barack and Michelle: Portrait of an American Marriage*, details a young couple with a growing family and highlights the unique stresses imposed by the intrusion of political ambition. Stories that particularly resonate with me are those of a wife in bed by 10 p.m. and her husband often up until 2 a.m., of a husband not pulling his weight with laundry or dirty dishes, and of an overachieving woman who bore the majority of the household's responsibilities while she cautiously witnessed her husband navigate the highs, lows, and grind of politics.

In fact, in the 2004 election for the Democratic nomination for the U.S. Senate, Barack Obama defeated my current opponent for Cook County Treasurer. He actually remains the last person to beat my opponent in any race since 2004. Given the votes I proudly cast for President Obama when he was on my ballot, it's thrilling to know that my name will appear on his ballot when he presumably votes in the March 2018 Illinois Democratic primary.

Another example that resonates is from a conversation that *The New Yorker*'s Mariana Cook had with Barack and Michelle Obama on May 26, 1996, as part of a photography project on couples in America. Michelle Obama was quoted as saying,

> When you are involved in politics, your life is an open book, and people can come in who don't necessarily have good intent. I'm pretty private, and like to surround myself with people that I trust and love. In politics you've got to open yourself to a lot of different people.

To which the young Barack replied,

> [W]hat sustains our relationship is I'm extremely happy with her, and part of it has to do with the fact that she is at once completely familiar to me, so that I can be myself and she knows me very well and I trust her completely, but at the same time she is also a complete mystery to me in some ways... It's that tension between familiarity and mystery that makes for something strong, because, even as you build a life of trust and comfort and mutual support, you retain some sense of surprise or wonder about the other person.

My wife is extremely outgoing and personable, while at the same time protective of the private life and home we are working to build for our family. Exceptionally articulate, thoughtful, tenacious, and intelligent without ever approaching pretentiousness, my wife is formidable. She is the most important person in my life. My candidacy was not her idea, or even her preference. She took a leap of faith over her apprehension with my involvement in politics and everything that comes with it, something for which neither of us was fully prepared.

There are countless evenings when both of us return home from a full day of work and chat for a minute or two about the day before she starts dinner for our daughter and I grab my same old sport coat and rummage through her purse for the key to our family car before opening the pantry for a snack that I can't spill on myself while driving and head out to the evening's list of campaign events. My wife does everything—and so many more things that I'll never know to thank her for doing. Dinner time, bath time, bedtime, bad dreams, temper tantrums, never-ending dishes and laundry, and everything else that comes with a toddler. Many times, I am ashamed to even ask how things went when I get home from another night of campaigning.

One of the greatest challenges in running for office is balancing my home life with the tempting simplicity of putting my head down and blindly charging forward into the campaign. In other words, to remain driven without driving away my loved ones. Without a break or much help from me, my wife singlehandedly carries the weight of our household. The strength she has revealed during my candidacy has become one of my greatest sources of motivation on the campaign trail. When we were married on October 20, 2012, we vowed to share the expected and the unforeseen responsibilities of a life together. As she solely carries the duties we committed to share, so that I may pursue an ambition that was never her preference, she deserves nothing less than my very best effort in this—and any other—endeavor.

My wife is also the reason I first moved to Chicago. During April 2008, I was living in Astoria, Queens, and was long overdue to visit my younger sister, who was a month from being graduated from Loyola University Chicago. My sister and I agreed on a weekend for a visit and after picking me up at Midway Airport, we headed to our cousin's apartment in Chicago's Lakeview neighborhood, not far from Wrigley Field, to start the weekend. It was great to see our cousin, but I was immediately distracted by her roommate, who my cousin had been friends with since their freshman year at Indiana University. We all headed out to the nearby Houndstooth Saloon, where my attempts to be witty came off as clumsy and misguided. To soothe my ego, I told myself, "Who cares? She lives in Chicago and I don't."

Back in Chicago a month later for Loyola's commencement, I reached out to my cousin's roommate to see if she was in town. We met up after my family went to dinner for my sister's big day. Luckily my nerves led to me shutting my mouth more than usual, which must have helped my chances because we ended up hitting it off. Over the next few months, we'd talk each day until eventually discussing longer-term plans. She made herself clear that she was not moving to New York—to which I reflexively and instinctively responded, "Okay. I'll move there."

The speed at which we went from meeting to living in the same city, to dating, to falling in love is a testament to "When you realize you want to spend the rest of your life with somebody, you want the rest of your life to start as soon as possible," a line from *When Harry Met Sally*, another love story that started in Chicago. My cousin still takes credit for introducing us, but I hold her accountable for us not meeting sooner.

❧

Neither life nor society guarantee one thing we should all have, which is unbiased access to the opportunity to pursue one's goals. I am not guaranteed to win my election, but I have access to the opportunity to run, and depending on my campaign, the opportunity to win and then contribute through public service. All members of society deserve the very same: access to opportunity, not just some token acknowledgement, but a real honest-to-goodness shot to get that job, to live where and how you want, or to get the education you want.

More than anything else, what I want for my daughter is fair access to the opportunity to chase her dreams. Whether she wants to be a chef, teacher, construction worker, engineer, physician, or whatever, her ability to access the necessary education and experience to reach her goals should be determined by her talent and work ethic, not by whether she or her family can afford tuition, or knows someone on an admissions panel, or has received a boost over someone else without comparable access to the same advantage. The world will be best served by my daughter if she earns her opportunities, takes advantage of them with her natural gifts and internal drive, and is qualified in the field where she desires to contribute. On that note, the world, and my daughter for that matter, will be disadvantaged if she's put in a position of power or privilege when she is not the most rightfully deserving candidate.

To achieve a more level playing field on which access to opportunity can be pursued more justly than today, I've identified five interwoven and complementary avenues of access to opportunity in this book:

- Education
- Fiscal Transparency
- Transportation
- Immigration
- Civic Engagement

What business does someone trying to be elected county treasurer have expressing his views on anything other than tax collection? The reason is that taxes are simply a means to funding the great things that government is capable of providing, but for government to do great things, which can often be very expensive, it must earn and keep the faith of taxpayers that their hard-earned tax dollars are not being wasted on misguided or corrupt undertakings. Government officials should aspire to instill pride in the act of paying one's taxes; almost like a home mortgage payment, where with every payment comes a greater stake in ownership. Taxpayers should be proud when they see a bridge being rebuilt or firefighter bravely charging into harm's way to help someone in need. Conversely, taxpayers should and often do feel anger when they learn of their tax dollars, under the stewardship of elected officials, being wasted by corruption, mismanagement or criminal activity. This is where the real value lies undisturbed in the office I am pursuing—to tirelessly work towards the ultimate, and maybe unreachable, goal of taxpayers being proud to pay their taxes because they received clear and actionable information from their county treasurer that led to electing officials who were competent and forward-thinking stewards of every tax dollar allocated by their budget votes. It may be quixotic to want transform a county treasurer's office into a spring from which taxpayer pride could eventually flow, but if I can spur any improvements, any steps toward generating the level of confidence taxpayers will need to comfortably fund transformational initiatives like the kind of high speed rail enjoyed in Europe and Asia or the level of education that every person in America deserves, well then, it will have all been worth the effort.

Why only identify five issues to push? I've always liked a concept articulated by Google's cofounder, Larry Page, of putting "more wood behind fewer arrows," which was one of Page's guiding philosophies during his tenure as Google's CEO, which led to record profitability. Personally, I am more likely to be productive in any endeavor if I work in a general direction and let the details and opportunities reveal themselves organically as I proceed. Jonathan Hutchison, a dear friend and former Amtrak colleague, frequently used the age-old expression "see the forest through the trees," meaning do not focus on minutiae that will limit the view and pursuit of your ultimate goal.

By focusing on just a handful of broader issues and supporting my positions with examples and policy proposals, I hope to lay out developed and defensible plans rather than more numerous shallow positions. Like Google's commitment under Larry Page to the growth of strategically chosen offerings, the five above-mentioned policy zones I will focus on in this book have both the capacity for generating public good and a high likelihood for containing undiscovered approaches to chronic challenges, such as inadequate access to quality education, to actionable financial information, to affordable and convenient transportation; a clear and compassionate immigration system; and increased civic participation. Each initiative deserves "more wood" in the form of an increasingly open-minded and concerted effort to uncover and implement new approaches and energy that will better serve the public through:

1. Offering affordable and effective education at the appropriate grade level;

2. Providing objective and helpful information explaining the value received for bearing the burden of taxes;

3. Safely and conveniently moving a growing number of people and goods through regions of growing population density;

4. Welcoming and supporting those who desire a chance in America; and

5. Involving people of every income level, zip code, and background in the institutions and decision-making processes that can affect and improve their lives and the lives of those they care about.

Progress is more often realized when efforts are integrated and working together under a common purpose, whether it is a kitchen staff preparing numerous multi-course meals, numerous contractors of different trades working at once to construct a building, or multiple areas of government seeking to improve life for those it exists to serve. By launching concurrent initiatives in the same general direction, unintended and desirable consequences will arise when those efforts grow organically into each other's paths and illuminate previously unconsidered solutions to long-standing problems. This panoramic approach to addressing several broad issues at once cultivates a landscape across which creative and connected solutions would not have otherwise come into being.

This book is about broad, overriding principles that are not only dear to me, but are also general directions that, when earnestly pursued with elbow grease and an open mind, can reveal solutions that will address multiple challenges at once. By embracing a teamwork approach in which concurrent government-led efforts complement each other, progress on a single issue can result in a high tide that lifts other efforts toward the wide-ranging objective of greater access to opportunity for all.

Chapter 2

Education

A ccess to opportunity can be improved by removing as many barriers as possible to receiving the highest-quality education possible. Traveling to, paying for, and remaining safe at school must never inhibit any individual's ability to receive the highest level of education that they desire to complete.

Jesuits are clergy members within the Catholic Church who belong to a congregation formerly known as the Society of Jesus. Whenever you see "SJ" after the name of a Catholic priest or brother, the initials stand for "Society of Jesus." Founded on September 27, 1540, by Saint Ignatius of Loyola, himself a reformed Spanish Basque soldier and ladies' man, the Jesuits emphasize education, serving the less fortunate, and finding God in all things. Jesuits regard knowledge as a treasure of humanity that can uplift and enhance the quality of the human experience and improve one's capacity to evaluate what is right, wrong, and negotiable.

A hallmark of Jesuit pedagogy is the concept of *cura personalis*, translated from Latin as "care for the whole person." A moral person unarmed with a quality education is unlikely to generate the impact they seek. A bright person without a wider point of view is likely to miss opportunities to expand his intellect and his network. People are multidimensional beings who become richer when open to new and challenging concepts and situations. Thus, the schools around the world operating in the spirit of Jesuit philosophy train and support students to expand their boundaries over a lifetime of engagement with culture, art, science, society, history, and other noble pursuits. I am the extraordinarily fortunate recipient of eleven consecutive years of Jesuit education, from seventh grade through graduate school.

In suburban Detroit, I attended the same small school from kindergarten until 1995, when after completing the 6th grade, my parents ended my predictable and comfortable cruise through school and, against my will, enrolled me at the University of Detroit Jesuit High School and Academy. Located off 7 Mile Road in Detroit, U of D Jesuit is an all-male school open since 1877. The academy was seventh and eighth grade, while the high school housed grades nine through twelve. At U of D Jesuit, expectations are high, the model is proven, and excuses are like rear ends: everyone has one and they all stink (an actual quote from a teacher).

At its population peak in 1950, approximately 2 million people resided in the sprawling 139-square-mile footprint of Detroit, Michigan. Both of my parents were born in Detroit during the 1950s, and both of their families left during the "white flight" to the suburbs in the wake of the 1967 riots. While many families, businesses and other institutions with roots in Detroit fled to the suburbs, on January 20, 1977, Fr. Douglas Keller, S.J., President of U of D Jesuit, announced that the school would "remain in the present location" and affirmed its commitment to "educational priorities of faith, academic excellence, community service, as well as racial and socio-economic diversity of the student body." Less than two decades later, I would be changed for the better by attending a school that knew all of its students benefited from diversity among their peers, as well as a rigorous curriculum.

After entering the imposing multistory limestone building on Detroit's northwest side as an anxious twelve-year-old to begin the 7th grade, I would leave six years later with my life on a trajectory that I could not have imagined. As a direct result of the student body's economic and ethnic diversity, dedication to community service, outstanding teachers, demanding workload, and the wise decision of my parents not to entertain my shortsighted initial protest, I was graduated as a confident young person with a greater awareness and empathy of the world beyond those who looked and sounded like me. It is not an overstatement to say that my parents' decision to send me to that school remains one of the best things they have ever done for me.

In the Austin neighborhood of Chicago's West Side, there are high school students receiving that same educational experience—not because their parents forced them, but because they each possess a work ethic and drive that I could not have fathomed at their age and cannot help but admire today. The remarkable students at Christ the King Jesuit College Preparatory School (CTK) not only endure demanding yet compassionate teachers, an unrelenting course load, extracurricular activities, and the infinite complexity of being a teenager, but they each balance all of those demands while working to cover 75 percent of the cost of tuition. The family income of an average CTK student, for a family of five, is less than $24,700. Every student is assigned a job in a professional environment, where they gain four years of exposure to highly skilled workers long before most of their peers will have experienced their first internship. With the support of their loved ones, each student does more than most their age to fund a high school experience that will materially alter the trajectory of their lives.

The Grad at Grad, short for Graduate at Graduation, is a list of five qualities that all Jesuit schools hope those who graduate possess by the time a degree is conferred:

1. Open to Growth
2. Intellectually Competent
3. Religious
4. Loving
5. Committed to Doing Justice

Schools under the Cristo Rey model, such as CTK, add the sixth quality of Work Experienced, since their students participate in the signature work–study program that not only helps fund the student's education, but provides invaluable exposure to a professional environment and empathy with those in the workforce.

A hallmark of Jesuit education is thoughtfully questioning the status quo in pursuit of a greater truth and/or justice. Knowing that the young people at CTK and other Jesuit schools are expanding their minds and hearts in the same educational tradition that has shaped countless leaders strengthens my confidence in these students who will undoubtedly be prepared to lead future generations as men and women for others.

In August 2001, my parents and I packed up the minivan with everything a college freshman thought he needed and made the 641-mile drive to the Bronx, New York City's only borough that is part of the contiguous United States. While we made trip after trip from the van to my dorm room in Hughes Hall at Fordham University, which I would share with three other guys (two from Connecticut and one from Idaho), my dad recalled a *Sports Illustrated* article that he had shared with me a few years earlier. Before the 1998 college football season, *Sports Illustrated* published a story on Andy Katzenmoyer, Ohio State's All-American middle linebacker starting his junior year. The article focused on Katzenmoyer's prodigious talent on the field, describing him as "6'4", 255 pounds, has run a 4.58 40, benches 450 pounds and closes on the football like Al Sharpton on a live microphone. 'He's a physical freak,' says Buckeyes coach John Cooper, 'and I mean that positively.'"

The article also highlighted Katzenmoyer's performance off the field, which included the then twenty-year-old being "pulled over two blocks from his apartment in Columbus and found to have a blood-alcohol level of .133, .033 over the legal limit in a state with a minimum drinking age of 21" and a sub-2.0 GPA.

The article went on to state that Katzenmoyer "comes, ironically, from a family that places a high value on higher learning." His mother "has undergraduate degrees in education and zoology, is an educational consultant and teaches at a community college; Andy's father, Warren, a wildlife biologist with a master's degree, is the budget administrator for Ohio's Division of Wildlife." When his mother was asked if her son's lack of attention to his studies bothered her, she replied, "Absolutely not. I always wanted my children to be able to do what they wanted to do, be able to express their excellence. We sent him to college to learn how to earn a living."

That was the point of my dad's story: "We sent him to college to learn how to earn a living."

My dad attended Colorado State University on a football scholarship from 1970–74. During spring practice in 1972 (his sophomore year), he was hit the wrong way and suffered a knee injury that would now be easily repairable but at the time was career-ending. Gone were any longshot hopes of playing for the Detroit Lions at Tiger Stadium or in their then-under-construction new home at the Pontiac Silverdome. Eager to maintain proximity to the athletic program, especially the football team, my dad became a sportswriter for the university's newspaper and a contributor to United Press International's sports newswire. He earned a bachelor's in political science and enrolled at Cooley Law School in Lansing, Michigan in Fall 1974. For my dad, that knee injury forced him to shift his focus from football to school and the acquisition of skills to generate a level of income with which he could support himself and his family. My dad still practices law in the Detroit area to this day.

Back to "We sent him to college to learn how to earn a living." As my parents unloaded the rest of the boxes and bags into my dorm room, my dad made it very clear that, like Andy Katzenmoyer, I was at college to learn how to make a living. (Unfortunately, Andy Katzenmoyer's NFL career never gained traction due to a chronic neck injury he suffered during his first season with the New England Patriots.)

Possessing average athletic talent, Andy Katzenmoyer's strategy entering college was not an option for me. Before my parents started the drive back to Michigan, my dad explicitly stated that I had four years or less to be graduated and find a full-time job or be accepted to a graduate program that would lead directly to a job, or on or before May 2005, or he would be driving me right back to my childhood bedroom. My mom added the requirement that I had to be a Resident Assistant (RA) for the maximum amount of time since RAs received room and board in exchange for being the primary contact between students living in campus housing and the university's office of residential life. Being an RA was actually one of my best college experiences. It allowed me to see the many layers of the university's bureaucracy hidden behind a curtain few other students were permitted. I learned which boundaries were acceptable to push with my superiors and how to better navigate the relationships with administrators of varying authority, and my fellow students for whose living situations I was responsible.

I love my parents, love the home they provided for my sisters and me, and love the area in which I was raised, but I knew without a doubt that I did not want to live again in my childhood bedroom because I had squandered the educational opportunity before me. My dad's words, or threat you could call it, helped motivate me to study when I otherwise would not have and influenced my decision-making on matters of material consequence.

As a student in the College of Business Administration, since renamed the Gabelli School of Business in recognition of a landmark gift made by alumnus and fund manager Mario Gabelli, I was required to take an introduction to financial accounting class as part of the core curriculum. Growing up without any accountants in my family, I held a stereotypical view of the profession, which, of course, included poor social skills and a green visor and pocket protector worn while hunched over an adding machine.

One day, the intro to financial accounting class was paused to introduce a recruiter from the accounting firm,

KPMG. The recruiter was good at his job and painted an exciting image of life as an accountant, specifically a Certified Public Accountant (CPA): "With offices in Honolulu, London, Hong Kong and elsewhere, a career at KPMG can lead to opportunities all over the world." It all sounded nice, but then he hooked me: "If your GPA is where we want it to be and you successfully complete our internship program after your junior year, you will have a full-time job offer, contingent on graduating and maintaining your GPA, to join the firm before you even start your senior year." I had not heard of any other major with such a direct and clear path to a job offer that would keep me from returning to my childhood bedroom. The recruiter left, class finished, and I walked over to the administration building to declare myself a Public Accounting major, not really knowing what it meant at the time, other than I had the motivation instilled by my dad to get the job the recruiter had just sold me.

At the heart of my college life was a diverse body of experiences made up of my field of study, living among fellow students as an RA, developing friendships with wonderful people of different ethnic, religious, cultural, and sexual backgrounds, and involving myself with a part of the country with which I previously had little familiarity. That collective experience contributed to a balanced education of my whole person, my *cura personalis*.

My parents set high educational and character expectations for their children and supported us in every way to meet those expectations. Born into the upper middle class, nothing I did gave me the right to be born into an objectively advantageous situation. Did I make the most of my opportunities and resources? At times, I definitely took my good fortune for granted and could have worked harder and smarter. My family provided a safety net at every step along the path of growing up, so even during what seemed like a failed attempt or an insurmountable challenge, my momentum and morale were never truly derailed. Did I deserve to be surrounded by an abundance of good fortune from the moment I entered the world? A more appropriate question is "What child does not deserve that situation?" How a child grows up matters. Put simply, the adult I am is due in large part to the child I was.

I am the beneficiary of a balanced educational diet that, unfairly, is not available to all students. The schools I attended never lost funding for the arts, athletics, updated textbooks, or other resources that I took for granted. Sufficiently staffed counseling departments; programs in music, philosophy, foreign language, and world religions; and access to up-to-date technology are all necessary to every student's intellectual arsenal as they each prepare to face a world of increasingly well-educated competition.

When my daughter was born, I began to see the world like my parents did when I arrived as their first child, and started to appreciate their wisdom and the sacrifices that bolstered my formative years. In becoming a father, I recognize that my child's success is more important than my own, no matter what my ambitions may be; so how can I help my child attain what she will consider to be "success"?

For now, my objective as a parent is to make sure she has the greatest level of access to opportunities that she wants to pursue. If, for example, she wants to be an astronaut, I want to make sure that she has access to the opportunity to take the necessary coursework in math and science to pursue that passion. Whether she has the talent and the work ethic to achieve that goal is up to her. My job as a parent—and society's responsibility for every child—is to make sure she can at least get to the point where it is up to her to succeed, fail, or to revise her objective.

Whether you have children, want them, or can barely tolerate them, each of us will be better off if we increase the odds that all children have unimpeded access to the opportunity to fulfill their potential. At the end of Disney's Pixar movie *Ratatouille*, the stuffy and suddenly enlightened restaurant critic writes, "Not everyone can become a great artist; but a great artist can come from anywhere." Our country should never stop doing everything possible to make certain that greatness never falls through the cracks because of a child's gender, family history, school district, race, economic status, or any other factor that should never work against a person. Every child is born with the potential to be great in one way or another, and deserves publicly-funded resources to make sure that potential is met.

In her insightful and encouraging book about the development of a child's brain, *Thirty Million Words*, Dr. Dana Suskind details the robust diet of nutritious words and conversation craved by a young mind. A pediatric ear surgeon, Suskind describes "[t]he wealth of untapped potential in people who never had a chance." Indeed, too many young minds, born into challenges beyond their control and that of their loved ones, never had a chance to avoid the pitfalls caused by socioeconomic conditions that persist in large part due to a lack of political will from elected officials on both sides of the aisle.

The Millennial generation, that has arrived into adulthood and is growing into leadership positions, must consciously take drastic measures to protect the potential greatness of younger generations that is too often lost to underinvestment in public education, public housing, affordable and nutritious food, and other essentials. As American adults and stewards of the standards for all people in our society, it should be a point of national pride to appropriately fund public education thought tax dollars to supply all students with the structure and support that could prevent losing the mind that will cure cancer or unlock cold fusion.

Members of any generation may scoff at paying high taxes, making shared sacrifices, and helping those they do not personally know and may not care about. It is the opportunity and responsibility of every taxing entity to help taxpayers understand how their tax dollars will benefit them and will not be wasted. The benefit to the skeptical taxpayer may be in the form of funding education and research, both of which might increase the odds of discovering a cure for a suffering loved one who otherwise would have not have had a chance without the work and talent of a person whose path had been supported by the tax dollars of taxpayer in question. The discovery of the technique or technology that could save lives may be waiting within the generation about to enter grade school. The odds of transformative discoveries being made increase if society as a whole makes an unprecedented commitment to investing in the education of all students, regardless of zip code, race, family income, or any other factor beyond an individual's control.

The world will continue to become more competitive and, as a nation, we cannot afford to let talent and promise, whether born or brought here, slip away. Bold and aspirational levels of sustained investment in education will be expensive. But the cost of maintaining the status quo or doing even less will be catastrophic to the economic and cultural health of our nation and its citizens. No expenditure of tax dollars is more important than the education of our youth at every level. Even our national defense will only be as strong as the minds of those brave enough to step forward and serve courageously.

Talent, brilliance, and work ethic cannot be bought or bound by the situation into which a person is born. The people who will have the greatest positive impact cannot be identified at birth, which means that as taxpayers, we must invest in and nurture every child, particularly those growing up in areas plagued by chronic violence, underemployment, and poverty. Good and talented children are in those neighborhoods, and we shall all suffer if every one of our children is not given sufficient access to the opportunity to learn and compete with their peers who were born into more supportive and better-resourced situations.

It was during my junior and senior years of college, that I was an RA. Part landlord, part counselor, an RA is the point of contact between those in student housing and the university's office of residential life. Not getting along with your roommate? Let's try to mediate. Your light is burned out? Let's call Facilities. Out of toilet paper? I've got the key to the storage closet. As a senior, I was an

RA for other upperclassmen who had already solved the riddles of college life that predominantly plague freshmen. As a junior, I was an RA to freshmen and witnessed first-hand the challenges that many faced during their first time away from the guidance and supervision of their childhood homes. The freshmen who struggled, some of whom didn't return for the spring semester, did not fail because they were stupid or lazy; in most cases they simply weren't ready to leave the direction and discipline of their parents' nest.

During the summer of 2003 before my junior year of collage, I participated in KPMG's externship program with other undergraduate accounting students from across the country. In my group were students from Brigham Young University (BYU) and the University of Utah. During our downtime, we would all talk, and it quickly became clear that the BYU and Utah students, all of whom were Mormon, were significantly more mature than the rest of us—certainly more mature than me. They were an average of two years older than the rest of us, due to their pause from college to serve their missions, which typically last two years for single men and eighteen months for single women. We all told each other how we ended up as accounting majors. For my Mormon peers, their decision to go into accounting was far more thoughtfully made, and often informed by the real-world experience gained during their missions. I felt lucky to have chosen a course of study that seemed to have a viable career path, but was slightly envious of the informed confidence the students from BYU and Utah had when making the decision to proceed with accounting. That relatively little bit of real-world experience empowered them during the pursuit of their chosen profession.

Fast forward to the end of 2003's fall semester when I was informed which of my freshman residents would not be returning for the spring semester. I wondered if those students on their way out would have benefitted from the perspective gained by immersion in the real world before or during college. Should those students have even been at the university in the first place, or were they just not ready? Were there more deserving students who would not have squandered the opportunity? Was it the fault of the admissions office for admitting incapable students in the first place? Was it the fault of the financial aid office for not offering adequate funding to more deserving and responsible applicants? Was it the fault of the alumni for not giving more for student financial aid? Maybe it was just the fault of individual teenagers who lacked self-discipline. Maybe there is more than enough blame to go around. However, could the university have enrolled a more promising crop of applicants if a student's ability to pay was not a consideration?

If every student enrolled in the best school they were accepted to, rather than the best school they could afford, imagine the extent to which that initiative could more fairly level the playing field while also serving our country's welfare. Perhaps a capable student would make a fantastic physician, but could not afford the requisite education. How many lives could that person have saved or improved if given the opportunity? If you are capable, you deserve the opportunity to better serve yourself, your family, your community, and your country. In doing so, your country will benefit over the long term from the wise investment in a bright and capable student. Put simply, there should exist a purer meritocracy that receives an aspirational level of public funding to advance the educational opportunity of all students for the good of all society.

How then can we move toward students being graduated from our best schools without the weight of educational debt that often stretches into middle age? How can we set in motion a system, or at least widely accessible options, so that future generations are more likely to enter the workforce unencumbered by the same levels of student debt that prevent many in my generation from starting their own business, buying a home, or taking other significant financial steps earlier than is common today? My answer to these questions began growing in the back of my mind—alongside the consciousness of my own student loan balance that was always back there too—when I was on a flight home for the holidays in 2003. I thought about what would have prepared those doomed freshmen who had failed out of school and would spend their holiday break finding a new school to accept them. Knowing there had to be a single stone that could hit the two birds of ballooning debt among college students and providing incoming college students with what would help them find a successful and productive path through college, I looked at multiple institutions with seemingly little in common for inspiration on how to pay for such an initiative.

My ideas began to coalesce: perhaps the answer is a taxpayer-funded work-study program concept wherein students earn their education through service. High school graduates would spend a year or two in service to the Red Cross, National Guard, AmeriCorps, or another government-affiliated organization. During that time, all participants would take college-level math, science, and English courses at a nearby location free of charge and for college credit. In taking a page from the United States service academies that require five years of active duty upon graduation, the work-study program would require three to four years of service after college or trade school, depending on the time contributed immediately after high school, in a field related to a college graduate's major to bring the total to five years committed.

After the initial year or two of service, the program would pay for the student to complete their educational track at:

1. An accredited public college or university (the program participant's state of residence does not matter, since participants will be encouraged to attend the best school they can get into regardless of cost or location);

2. An accredited private college or university; or

3. An accredited trade school, vocational school, technical training institution, or apprenticeship program.

Should a participant drop out of school, the money they earned from the taxpayer-funded work-study program toward their education would stay with the school, or be transferred to another accredited school in which the student has enrolled, to encourage students to finish their degree and to prevent participating schools from being shortchanged.

The idea, while certainly not perfect, pulls inspiration from:

1. Those countries in which college is free, such as Norway, Finland, Sweden, Germany, Slovenia, and France. Once again, just imagine if an entire country's students attended the best colleges and universities to which they were admitted without

financial consideration. In less than a generation, America could benefit from a deeper pool of educated innovators and skilled workers fueling economic growth upon domestically cultivated knowledge.

2. The Mormon missionary program in which college-age men and women are sent into the real world, potentially exposing them to a professional path that otherwise might have not been considered. Perspective gained through experience often has the greatest impact and duration. Just a year or two in the real world after high school could make one's time in college or a vocational program more informed and lead to students pursuing higher education with a more defined vision of where they want to go.

3. The Cristo Rey model of students gaining valuable experience in the workplace, as well as in the classroom, generates positive exposure to a skilled work environment that can guide and motivate one's educational path. The Cristo Rey Corporate Work Study Program requires high school students to experience viable career paths years before they would typically think about the sort of job likely to be available once they complete their education. Receiving such an opportunity in one's teenage years provides

real-world perspective on available paths that could match interest with academic capability and put a student on a more productive and enjoyable track well before many of their peers approach that level of clarity.

The primary goals of this taxpayer-funded work-study concept would be to minimize and ultimately eliminate student loan debt, endow college graduates with the experience-driven perspective of public service, and better empower students to find their way into a field of preference and opportunity to combat the likelihood of bringing a degree with low demand into an unsympathetic job market. To be clear, this proposed program would be entirely voluntary. Should a student want to go straight from high school to college, that option should not be limited in any way. The program would be for graduating high school seniors of any income level who wish to fund their education and gain real-world experience earlier than they normally would on a traditional college path, through the commitment of time to public service.

〜〜

Aaron Sorkin, creator of the television drama "The West Wing," said it best when one of the show's characters, Sam Seaborn, showed his true feelings about the importance of education:

[E]ducation is the silver bullet. Education is everything. We don't need little changes, we need gigantic, monumental changes. Schools should be palaces. The competition for the best teachers should be fierce. They should be making six-figure salaries. Schools should be incredibly expensive for government and absolutely free of charge to its citizens, just like national defense.

Answering the noble call of teaching should not require consent to financial martyrdom, and every single school should be a temple of knowledge, security, encouragement, and tolerance. Too much is demanded of and too little is given to the teachers who directly shape the minds and collective conscience of our nation's future. The professionals who dedicate their careers to education should be compensated in accordance with the weight of their responsibility.

Appropriately compensating teachers should take place immediately, and before implementing another necessary change to our educational system, which is the year-long school year.

Prior to the widespread availability of air conditioning, schools were too warm to remain in session during the summer months. As families of means escaped the summer's swelter to destinations away from their children's schools, school administrators acquiesced, and the concept of summer vacation was solidified. According to Kenneth Gold, Associate Professor and Dean of the School of Education at the College of Staten Island, "By the late 19th century, school reformers started pushing for standardization of the school calendar across urban and rural areas. So a compromise was struck that created the modern school calendar." In short, the school year as we know it today was not designed with student development as its priority.

During the traditional summer vacation period of Memorial Day to Labor Day, students, on average, lose a full month of knowledge, better known as "the summer slide." Summer vacation has a more pronounced negative effect on those children whose families cannot afford the education and supervision that comes from costly trips, camps, tutors, and activities from June through August.

Since July 1997, a grade school in the Chicago suburb of Des Plaines has combatted summer slide as a year-round school. Iroquois Community School is the longest-standing year-round public school in the Chicago area. The school's approximately 500 students are in class for just as many days—174—as students enrolled in the school district's other schools that operate under the traditional school-year calendar. However, at Iroquois the required days of instruction are spread over the entire calendar. The year-round school year, which is credited with higher rates of academic performance and student retention, begins in mid-July, has a three-week break in the fall, a two-week break around the winter holidays, a three-week spring break, and a six-week break in the summer. During each of those breaks, families can pay out of pocket for students to take classes on elective topics not offered in the standard curriculum or to receive additional attention throughout the year in an area of weakness to make sure a student has a better chance of remaining on pace with their classmates.

Today's students are not just competing with peers across their state or part of the country. They are in college applicant pools with talented and driven students from all over the world, similarly eager to earn an education from a recognized college or university. To better prepare our children, not only for college, but also for the global competition they will face when entering the workforce, every available advantage, such as year-round schooling, should be thoughtfully pursued.

To attract and retain the best possible teachers, accommodate year-round learning, and adequately resource every public school, voters must demand that elected officials establish and defend aspirational and consistent levels of funding for public education. Put simply, it is virtually impossible to overinvest in the education of our youth.

❧

Income inequality and the resulting plague of poverty remains as great a challenge as ever for young minds and their families. Without adequately resourced schools and support systems, these students and families will move from one struggle to the next, while more fortunate students and families leap, on schedule, from one milestone to another. In a just society, which ours is not, hard work and talent would be the only things standing between a person and the viable pursuit of their desired path, but today the assignment of difference-making resources often has more to do with the family a person is born into, rather than the natural gifts and drive inside that individual.

In September 2011, National Public Radio produced a piece called "Making It in the U.S.: More Than Just Hard Work." The article featured the research of Brandeis University Professor Tom Shapiro, who over the course of more than thirty years observed families of different racial and economic backgrounds and concluded that inheritance is a primary factor in the wealth gap between races.

The inheritance gap disproportionately affects Americans of color and must be addressed. As long as that gap continues to impact who is likely to be empowered with a quality education and who is likely to be deprived of one, we as a society will shortchange our fellow citizens, succeeding generations, and ourselves— at least as long as we allow elected officials to sustain policies that preserve a system in which a person's odds for a quality education, and everything that it can lead to, is overly and unjustly weighted by a family's wealth and skin color.

Inheritance, both the value of assets passed down and the time over which money had grown, unsurprisingly and overwhelmingly favors white families. In short, once you are rich, it is easier to keep yourself and your family rich—or at least out of poverty. As of 2016, the average white family possessed 7 times the wealth of the median black family. If a child of color starts off with less of a chance of his or her family being able to help afford college, start a business, or buy a home than the family of a white child, the child of color will permanently play catch-up rather than compete on a more level playing field. Inequity perpetuated by the growing racial disparity in wealth fuels an achievement gap that has an increasingly detrimental effect on students, their families, and our societal well-being.

I am not criticizing the ability to earn income and provide for loved ones into the future. I am saying that inheritance should not be an overriding factor that determines a child's likelihood to obtain an education that will allow that child to grow into a person equipped to compete and contribute in the modern workforce.

⁓

For every child, the experience of school should be evermore safe, comfortable, and encouraging. Steve Chapman of the *Chicago Tribune* wrote in June 2015 that "[c]hildren who feel unsafe at school, who are disproportionately black, do measurably worse academically. Those who witness shootings or suffer violent attacks may develop posttraumatic stress disorder." Chapman's point was supported by Princeton University sociologist Douglas Massey, who stated that "people who are exposed to high levels of stress over a prolonged period of time are at risk of having their brains rewired in a way that leaves them with fewer cognitive resources to work." Having fewer cognitive resources makes it more difficult to do the things commonly considered to be fundamental, such as completing high school, getting a job, and evaluating potential long- and short-term consequences before making decisions.

Chapman went on to mention a truth that remains present, but often goes unstated: simple tales of grit from past generations are not applicable to overcoming chronic gun violence, poverty, and underinvestment that punishes many poor urban areas with predominantly nonwhite populations. On their own, elbow grease and a nose to the grindstone have not been enough for a long time now, particularly in those areas with obstacles spanning multiple generations where children are unreasonably expected to grow into adults who can compete with those who never feared for their safety, questioned the source of their next meal, or doubted that working hard and doing the right thing would be enough to get ahead.

Tragically, home is not a consistently dependable refuge for every child. For every student to experience and view school as a sanctuary, public school buildings in high-risk communities should receive taxpayer dollars to remain open and secure twenty-four hours a day with social workers and security personnel on hand so that children will always have a dependable, safe option. A similar idea was proposed by the U.S. Attorney for the Northern District of Illinois. Before departing office in March 2017, Zachary Fardon drafted a letter to his staff about the challenges, opportunities, and experiences encountered during his time as the Obama Administration's U.S. Attorney in Chicago from October 23, 2013, to March 13, 2017. In his letter, Fardon suggested the potential impact on a neighborhood safe haven for Chicago's youth at the highest risk of committing or being victimized by gang-related violence, urging the city to:

> [C]reate new youth pathway centers, in the handful of most afflicted neighborhoods, that are not subject to the shifting winds of politics and government. The kids in our hardest hit neighborhoods are gang affiliating as young as 10, 11, 12 years old. Once that's happened, it's too late; their fate is sealed.

Mr. Fardon further laid out the importance of a safe haven for youth in at-risk neighborhoods:

> To do that, we should have a brick and mortar place, in each afflicted neighborhood, that is base,

the home, the epicenter to that effort. No different than combining our federal law enforcement resources makes sense, combining our social services resources to maximize impact in these neighborhoods makes sense. There are smart and passionate social services workers out there right now, every day, trying to help. But no different than our police, systemic deficiencies are making it impossible for them to succeed.

Brick and mortar. Create a place. Call it anything. Fund it with federal, state, or philanthropic funds, or some combination. But do not continue this madness of annualized state or federal grant funding to where all these not-for-profits have time to do is fight for those peanuts, compete with each other and hope to survive. That serves no one.

There is plenty of money and good will in this town. And there are millions of federal dollars spent across this town every year. So let's find that money and put it to use by creating youth centers, brick and mortar, funding social workers and experts, and intervening to save the lives of kids and young adults.

Children, particularly those in at-risk situations, deserve a safety net, a place of refuge at which they can always find shelter and security. No child is born bad. No child deserves to feel scared or pressured into making an uncomfortable choice because it is their least worst option. Brick-and-mortar locations that are well resourced, thoughtfully designed, and strategically located could make the difference for a child who otherwise might not be able to escape the pressure or solitude that leads to a destructive decision.

As taxpayers, we should fund daring and groundbreaking efforts to uphold and advance the principles of justice and equality upon which our nation was founded. All of our children deserve to have everything they need to grow up and offer society their best, and it is long overdue for we taxpayers to demand whatever we need to confidently provide the resources to support the minds that are at-risk within our future generations.

Chapter 3

Fiscal Transparency

Access to opportunity can be improved by enhancing a person's ability to more efficiently retrieve information that leads to move effective advocacy for one's own priorities. Without access to clear and actionable information, the path of advocacy is unilluminated by fact and increasingly susceptible to a backward slide into unproductive frustration.

One of my favorite writers has always been Shel Silverstein. His classic book, *Where the Sidewalk Ends*, is a collection of children's poetry, with one exception. Silverstein wrote the book's namesake poem for adults. The second stanza reads:

Let us leave this place where smoke blows black
And the dark street winds and bends.
Past the pits where the asphalt flowers grow
We shall walk with a walk that is measured and slow,
And watch where the chalk-white arrows go
To the place where the sidewalk ends.

Addressing the Irish Government's Dáil on June 28, 1963, President Kennedy said, "George Bernard Shaw, speaking as an Irishman, summed up an approach to life, 'Other people,' he said, 'see things and say why? But I dream things that never were and I say, why not?'"

President Kennedy and Shel Silverstein, each in his own way, articulated the importance of always being open to the power of creativity. Constant creativity is particularly important in public service, where elected officials must concurrently make difficult decisions and discover new ways to extract more and more value for taxpayers at less cost. The task before voters is to elect capable and creative candidates who will approach an office's challenges from new and unique angles.

Within municipal offices and the local elected officials who lead those offices is the key that begins to unlock the taxpayer confidence that will be essential to realizing large transformative initiatives that must eventually come from the federal level. Before we can realize the benefits of other bold and creative programs that can level barriers to more equitable access to opportunity, taxpayer trust must first be further cultivated at the level of government with which people have the most intimate and frequent relationship, and that is their local government. Before government can ask more of taxpayers, it must first give them peace of mind that they are receiving adequate value in return for bearing their tax burden.

∿

From 2011 to 2016, my wife worked for a company that sent her to meetings and conferences in cities around the world. When my schedule allowed, I would meet her halfway through the trip for sightseeing and a day or two of vacation. In August 2013, she had to go to Zurich, Switzerland, so I tagged along. Our hotel was a small and clean example of efficient European space management, walking distance from most of the city's tourist spots, and along a road with a streetcar on the route into downtown. Sleeping with our window open, we'd hear the endless chime of the streetcars that seemed to run at all hours. One morning, I mentioned to a hotel worker how impressively frequent their street cars were and how beautifully their city was kept. With an expression that said this was not the first time she'd received a compliment on behalf of Zurich, she said "We pay enough in taxes, so at least we can see where the money is going."

That hotel worker's view on high taxes made an impression on me. Her tax bill was high, but she was comfortable with it—not necessarily happy—because the amount paid was in line with her expectations for the level of public service delivered. Switzerland has a progressive income tax system, meaning the tax rate rises as the amount subject to tax goes up, which leads to a fairer system of revenue generation whereby those who have more pay more and those of more modest means pay a more reasonable share. That Swiss hotel worker did not like paying taxes any more than you or I do, but what she did have was the comfort of knowing that her money was not being wasted and that she was benefited from how her tax dollars were used by her government.

A year and a half later, in April 2015, the seed planted by the Swiss hotel worker's comment sprung up when I saw the Obama Administration's Taxpayer Receipt that illustrated how one's 2014 federal taxes were spent by the federal government. This fresh, simple, and logical idea spoke to me as a move toward educating taxpayers and inducing greater civic engagement with elected officials. For example, a constituent telling an elected official that taxes are too high is not terribly useful feedback. But if that same constituent said, "For the most recent tax year, too much of my money went toward a certain aspect of Program A, and not enough went to a particular feature of Program B. Thus, please introduce or support legislation that would accordingly adjust federal spending." With a greater amount of information and context coming from a more informed taxpayer, the elected official can more effectively represent a constituent's priorities and solicit more valuable feedback from other constituents to better gauge the collective mood of the city, county, district, or state.

Improving access to opportunity through the interconnected strands of education, fiscal transparency, transportation, immigration, and civic engagement is sort of a chicken-and-egg issue. An immigrant who relies on a poor public transit system for transportation could be limited in her access to a job that would be needed to support a work visa and the path to naturalization. A person who pays increasingly high local taxes and is dissatisfied with the resources allocated to his child's public school will have an extremely difficult time advocating for changes that could improve his child's education without transparent, detailed, and easily digestible information that generate a specific and informed request for the person's elected official. It all ties together, but I believe the first step in improving these paths to equal access to opportunity has to be enhancing the availability of actionable taxpayer information.

For government to do the big, great things that only government can do, such as transformative, large-scale infrastructure, public education, and immigration reform, people must trust the government's ability and sincerity to efficiently and fairly carry out those initiatives that are beyond the scope of the private sector. Before the government can earn the people's trust, it must first combat distrust and suspicion that tax dollars are routinely subject to corruption, incompetence, and waste.

Change starts with solid useful information. Without it, how can you develop a specific and measurable request that will lead to meaningful progress on any front? As citizens, we should seek to put our elected officials in the position to best represent the interest of their constituents and to be held accountable for their actions. We should always ask more of our elected officials. By providing them with more detailed and informed requests, voters can better judge whether they are being represented to their satisfaction.

"Taxes have proven to be an irritant since the days of the American Revolution, yet are the best way to provide for the common good, which is a moving target," said Cook County Judge Daniel Kubasiak during the contentious 2017 implementation of an additional sales tax on sugary drinks in Cook County. The tax eventually was repealed due to overwhelming public opposition, but Kubasiak's comment remains right on the money (pun intended). Elected officials and the public should cooperatively pursue the "moving target" for the highest and best use of taxes. That pursuit will be most efficient and productive if the public, as an essential partner, has actionable, objective information upon which they can direct and inform their elected officials.

Currently, a Cook County taxpayer who wants to see how their household is directly served by their property tax dollars has to assemble information from all layers of their respective taxing districts. In one place, taxpayers (renters and property owners) should see how many of their tax dollars went to their child's school, to the park near their home, to the police district that responds to emergencies, or to other hyper-local services and amenities. In other words, residents should be able to see what they are specifically getting for their rising taxes.

To be clear, any information not provided in a useful format is done so needlessly. Do not let anyone mislead you into believing that you cannot understand how your tax dollars align with your priorities, because you can and you absolutely should. When I go in for my annual physical, the doctor doesn't just hand me a sheet with the results of my blood work and say, "Here, I'm being transparent." Instead, the doctor uses the raw data to objectively inform me in a clear and useful way that empowers me with information about my health. Taxpayers deserve the same useful transparency on their taxes.

Understandably, no one is happy with any bill, whether it's for groceries, utilities, or property taxes. But with a clear connection between money paid and value received, it is possible to be more comfortable with a bill. Whether you buy one item at the grocery store or a whole cartful, you can read your itemized receipt and clearly see what

Who Among Giants

you received for your money. You might feel that the price of a particular item is too high, but you likely do not feel robbed by the entire grocery store. This kind of unbiased transparency on municipal spending is the first step toward the larger goal of increasing taxpayer comfort with and approval of how tax dollars are expended and benefits returned to the public.

❧

During my campaign, on August 15, 2017, I went to the Englewood neighborhood of Chicago's South Side, where Cook County Clerk David Orr was holding a public event to encourage voter participation. Orr holds his own place in Cook County political lore. As the former alderman of Chicago's 49th Ward, he was vice mayor when Harold Washington, Chicago's first African-American mayor and a progressive icon whose service and story inspires to this day, died suddenly of a heart attack, seven months into his second term at the age of sixty-five while at his desk in City Hall. Unexpectedly ascending to Chicago's top job, Orr deftly and without self-interest navigated a spike in the city's political and civil unrest. Serving just a week as mayor, he returned to his position as an alderman on the City Council before eventually being elected county clerk in 1990.

It was at that August 2017 event in Englewood that I first met Orr. He fielded an interesting question from a man in the audience that evening: "What am I getting for my vote?" The obvious answer was a voice to be heard in deciding who will represent you in the different layers of government, but the man asked again and emphasized the literalness of his question. "I understand why I should vote, but I've been voting for years and don't know if I am being helped or hurt by the person I vote for or against, so how can I know what I am getting for my vote?" That question captured what needed to be advanced: to objectively quantify the answer to what people are getting for their vote. I had to bite my tongue to keep from immediately thanking the man out loud for so succinctly articulating a key tenet of my young campaign.

People should know what they are getting for their tax dollars and, by extension, for their vote. How you are taxed and how your dollars are used are elemental functions of any government; thus, how your representatives vote on budgets that appropriate funds to your priorities is an objective and clear way to answer what you are getting for your vote. While certainly not the only way to judge an elected official, it is a fair and clear way for voters to hold their officials accountable with useful and unbiased information. To the man in a t-shirt standing in the back of the ground-floor room at Life Builders United on South Emerald Avenue in Chicago on the evening of August 15, 2017, thank you for your question!

President Obama's Taxpayer Receipt, which I mentioned earlier, would have gone a long way to showing voters like that man what he gets for his votes. It made perfect sense to provide individuals with a detailed and useful breakdown of how their income taxes are allocated by the federal government. As a CPA who does individual tax work, I had never seen this level of useful transparency offered to taxpayers by the government. The website, which is archived at https://obamawhitehouse. archives.gov/2014-taxreceipt, invited taxpayers to enter their Social Security Tax withheld, Medicare Tax withheld, and Income Tax, then hit "calculate" to see what they contributed, down to the dollar, to Health Care and subcategories like Medicaid and Medicare, and to National Defense and its subcategories of ongoing operations, research, and development, and so on. It continued with line items for Job and Family Security, Veterans Benefits, International Affairs, Agriculture, and so forth.

With this easily digestible presentation of how my tax dollars were used in the tax year in question, I could call my Representative or Senator and state my preference for reducing my overall tax bill by decreasing spending in a specific area or advocate for a shift in funds from one initiative to another or even suggest that my taxes should increase to provide additional resources to an issue dear to me. Most people regularly interact with how their local tax dollars are spent more so than federal spending. Public schools, local roads, parks, emergency services, and other amenities in Cook County are primarily funded by local property taxes. Like many, I am particularly concerned with the potholes in my neighborhood, the resources that support first responders in my community, the public schools my toddler daughter will one day attend, and the nearby park that my family and I utilize.

Inspired by the Obama Administration's idea, I wanted to know how many of my property tax dollars were going not into the overall Chicago Park District budget, but to the specific park my family uses most. I wanted to know how many of my tax dollars are going not just to the Board of Education, but to the public schools that someone living at my address could attend. With information of that ease and clarity on the issues that matter most to me, I and every other taxpayer could see the direct connection between what we pay and how our respective household is served by those tax dollars.

Why can't we do this?

We are not prevented by a force of nature or technology that does not exist. This is a problem of will and creativity, and the solution is political. As a taxpayer, if you are not happy with how your money is spent or what you receive in return for what you pay, the problem is not with the tax, it is with the person or persons elected to serve you. You deserve more with every dollar you pay in taxes and from every politician who wants your vote. Don't give either away without being able to know what you are getting in return.

It is in taking the concept of useful transparency a step further that I have to once again thank that gentleman for asking "What am I getting for my vote?" For your vote on a legislative office, you are getting an elected official charged with representing your interest during the budgeting process. Tax dollars do not allocate themselves. They go only where they are appropriated by a budget that is voted on and approved. At the local, state, and federal levels, every American is represented by a least one elected official in the respective budgeting processes. Therefore, there is a direct connection that should be emphasized and made as clear as possible between how well your tax dollars serve your household and how well you are represented on decisions about how to use your tax dollars.

Improving the information communicated through tax bills should be an endlessly iterative process not only to deliver, but to discover new value for taxpayers. After all, a car company would never say, "Well, we've made a good sedan, and now we're done until we receive complaints about this model." My belief in the good that could come from increased civic engagement induced by highlighting the immediate bond between your taxes and your vote is a key reason for why I decided to run for the office that issues the property tax bills for my county's 1.8 million parcels and has the greatest opportunity to offer taxpayers an unprecedented level of useful transparency.

Put simply, I want people to feel a sense of pride in paying their taxes because they more wholly understand how they benefit from the taxes they pay. Certainly, other required duties are known to engender more civic pride, such as registering for the Selective Service System or participating in jury duty, so why shouldn't patriotism spring from meeting one's financial obligation to their government?

Marketing government debt to the public was a concept pioneered by the British in 1751. The U.S. Congress first financed America's armed forces with debt during the War of 1812. World War II remains the last time the United States explicitly issued the finance instrument commonly known as a war bond, which many citizens purchased out of a sense of duty and patriotism to "support the troops" and "defend your country with your dollars."

Fortunately, we are not in the midst of another world war (knock on wood), yet a similar sense of pride that was present during the purchase of a war bond is not there when paying one's income or property taxes. While the difference may be partially attributed to wartime solidarity, my guess is that the explicit nature of war bonds gave people comfort as to how their money would benefit an issue they supported.

While purchasing war bonds were an elective disbursement compared to mandatory tax payments, the lesson to be learned is that the simplest way to generate pride from paying taxes is to help people be proud of where their money is going. To do that, we need to start at the local level, where each of us interacts most closely with the services and amenities funded by tax dollars. Ideally, each person would nod with a sense of ownership when seeing their money at work every time they see a police officer on patrol, a fire truck speeding to a call, or a public school receiving students in the morning.

Before people can be proud to pay their share of taxes, they must no longer be skeptical of whether the value they receive reasonably correlates to the amount they pay. Greater comfort with how existing tax dollars are generating a direct or indirect return for taxpayers will only help to diminish resistance to just and necessary tax decisions.

I've always gotten a kick out of unique and creative mascots, particularly college mascots, and there's one that I prefer. There are tons of schools with rams or wildcats, such as my alma maters—and how about those Banana Slugs of the University of California at Santa Cruz, the Mastodons of Indiana University–Purdue University Fort Wayne, or the Ephs of Williams College. But of all the unconventional mascots, my favorite is from the oldest school west of the Mississippi River, which also happens to be a Jesuit school: the Billiken of Saint Louis University. The university describes a billiken as "a mythical good-luck figure who represents 'things as they ought to be.'" While it is a one-of-kind mascot, the billiken's approach is far from pragmatic. Admittedly, my desire to effect change through the political system is somewhat quixotic; still, I accept that I must embrace and operate within the political system as it stands today in order to be a serious candidate who can effect positive change.

I fully understand that I am running for office within a system that requires a specific skill set and a commitment to raising money. Knowing that, I still chose to run within the system, and I am running to win.

But over the course of my campaign, it's become clearer to me that fundraising is a deceptively inaccurate measurement of political acumen and ability to perform once in office. Privately-sourced campaign dollars make the voters' job more difficult by allowing candidates to paper over shortcomings that will be unavoidably revealed once in office, where support from donors will not offer the cover that could be purchased on the campaign trail.

I believe in my reasons for running more than I might disagree with any part of the political process. So, with eyes wide open and no request for sympathy, I will work and fight for my beliefs within the system as it exists, not as I would like it to be. If I am fortunate enough to earn a position that can improve the system, well, you can be damn sure that I will do as much as possible with any opportunity.

Because our current system is nuts.

Improvements must be made to the accessibility of the political process so that the best possible person for every elected office is more likely to step forward and realistically compete without previous notoriety or access to financial wealth. It is in the best interest of all residents and all layers of government that the best possible candidates are drawn to serve and compete in a political process that never stops moving each elected office closer to optimization, without regard for the tenure of an incumbent. In other words, our political system should shift its focus from the official to the office and the public that office exists to serve.

The political process should perpetually iterate in order to emphasize every candidate's demonstration of the corresponding skills necessary to do the job—not to run a successful campaign, but to successfully serve in the office being pursued. A candidate's fundraising ability does not correlate with an elected official's potential or likelihood to affect meaningful change. For example, my ability to fundraise might help my odds of getting elected, but if I win, it will not be a skill that helps me execute the office; therefore, the demonstration of that skill should be intentionally minimized in order to better highlight the qualities most likely to add value for voters.

The current system of campaign financing, in which candidates must self-fund, and/or solicit funds from corporate entities and individuals, obscures voters' ability to decide which candidate deserves their vote at the end of a campaign that should be more like a job interview and less like a telethon. With public financing of campaigns, and identical budgets imposed upon all candidates in a race by the governmental body supervising the election, political campaigns could better showcase each candidate's ability to adhere to a fixed budget—a demonstrable skill that is universally applicable in any elected office. Unfortunately, the current campaign finance system at the federal level, and in most states, deters and prevents the regular replenishment of a talented pool of potential candidates.

People should be of equal value in the eyes of those aspiring to represent them. In other words, candidates and elected officials should not be incentivized to focus more on one group or individual over another in order to improve the chance of securing a financial campaign contribution. Elected officials, candidates and voters deserve the opportunity to perform their duties under the freedom and clarity afforded by publicly financed campaigns that could finally remove money with strings attached from our electoral process.

❧

The average voter has a job, responsibilities around the home, interests that extend well beyond politics, and a life to live. Therefore, in the interest of voters, the playing field for all candidates, incumbents and challengers alike, should be as level as possible. If a candidate is able to stand out in a voter's eyes, the voter can have peace of mind of knowing that the candidate earned that visibility on the merits of his or her platform or political talent with the same quantifiable resources on hand as the rest of the field.

All of this leads to the conclusion that we should publicly finance campaigns, which would:

1. Provide the best, most helpful information to voters and minimize factors that don't help them evaluate a candidate's likely effectiveness in office.

Unlimited funds in politics makes the job of voters more difficult. Money can mask a candidate's laziness, poor preparation, or lack of financial management skills. Money also can weaken a talented candidate by diverting too much of the candidate's time to fundraising and away from voter contact.

In a campaign finance system where all candidates have the same resources, personal wealth and the advantages and disadvantages that can accompany it are rendered moot, just as the effect of personal wealth would be, should the candidate be elected. Most important, voters would be more likely to elect the optimal candidate for the job.

2. Improve the system to seek the best, most innovative, and most effective candidates who have the greatest chance to win, not just the person who can raise the most money, often from special interests or from those who have business before the governmental entity.

As candidates, we waste so much time raising money by soliciting people with enough disposable income to give to a political campaign—donors who will in all likelihood be able to live how they want with minimal dependence on government-provided services that will have a far greater impact on individuals of more modest means.

Voters deserve (and our government needs) officeholders who focus on the job they were elected to do more than on the next election. Wealth is not a qualification for elected office; nor is it a disqualification. With no correlation between personal wealth and effectiveness at any level of government, steps should be taken to make it easier for voters to see the meaningful flaws a candidate could cover up with enough money.

If our brightest, most engaged, and most energized citizens knew they could step forward and compete on equal footing against a career politician or a wealthy first-time candidate, if the content of someone's heart and head and not their wallet or donor base began to make the difference in our elections, just imagine the positive shift in our political system that could occur.

3. Bring more citizens into the political process, because the current system of financing campaigns skews our democracy by leading

people to assume politicians are bought-off by wealthy individuals and special interests.

Mandatory participation in public financing for all candidates would help ensure that existing officeholders are focused on public service rather than on fundraising for the next cycle. If the money to fund a candidate's campaign is coming only from a single traceable public origin, there will be a significant reduction in potential conflicts of interest and trading favors in office for financial contributions. The fastest way to get rid of dirty politicians is to get rid of dirty money in politics.

With all of the noble and useful activities that tax dollars could be used for, should campaigns for political candidates be one of them? Absolutely. If elected, those candidates will have control over how a far greater amount of tax dollars are collected and used. Thus, it is in the best interest of taxpayers to invest in a process that helps identify and elect the best possible candidate for a particular office. While not a silver bullet, a current program in the State of Connecticut helps provide a more level footing from which voters can decide for whom to vote. Administered by the Connecticut State Elections Enforcement Commission, The Citizens' Election Program is a voluntary public campaign financing program that exists to reduce the influence of private money in the state's political process and to encourage greater participation among qualified candidates interested in running for statewide office or the General Assembly.

The cliché of getting what you pay for applies to politics as well. For political donors able to consistently give large amounts, you can bet they receive a higher level of access to candidates and elected officials than a small-dollar contributor or a nongiving constituent. After all, why would a high-dollar donor keep coming back with more money only to receive the same treatment as someone who gave nothing? A high-dollar donor gets what they pay for often enough to continue giving the big money.

Being a primarily self-funded candidate does not always guarantee electoral success. For every Dave Bing (two-term mayor of Detroit and Naismith Hall of Fame basketball player) or Michael Bloomberg (three-term mayor of New York City), there is a Ross Perot (unsuccessful presidential candidate in 1992 and 1996), Meg Whitman (unsuccessful candidate for governor of California in 2010), Steve Forbes (unsuccessful presidential candidate in 1996 and 2000), and Linda McMahon (unsuccessful candidate for U.S. Senate in Connecticut in 2010 and 2012). While a self-funding candidate would, in theory, not be beholden to a high-dollar donor whom they never had to approach for support, they risk not sharpening or exhibiting the political skills of a more seasoned or talented opponent because they feel they can simply outspend an opponent who must take time away from the campaign trail to fundraise. This should be taken with a grain of salt, since I have personally provided most of the relatively modest budget for my current campaign.

Of course, some self-funded candidates who won their races and served as decent and productive elected officials were capable of winning without their wealth. However, for those victorious self-funders whose wealth overwhelmed their electorate into a poor choice, it is the public that suffers because of the unchecked ability to use private personal wealth to affect the voting public's decision.

Imagine a marathon between two runners, one rich and one not rich. The marathon has no rules regarding equipment, performance-enhancing drugs, or a support team. The race just has a starting line, a finish line, and few other rules of consequence. The rich runner has special shoes that minimize fatigue, regularly takes anabolic steroids, and runs with a support team that provides pacing, refreshments, and cheers of encouragement. The not-rich runner has regular shoes from a local sporting goods store and nothing more. Both runners are on the same course and will start and end at the same points to cover the same distance. With no guarantee the rich runner's advantage will result in victory, what are we to make of their advantages? While the hope remains that the better runner will win regardless of who's better resourced, experience makes us doubtful.

The other side of getting what you pay for comes to the taxpayers, whether it is the quality of our transportation infrastructure or the type of people we have serving in elected offices at all levels of government. Under the current system, those candidates who cannot afford to self-fund, which is a vast majority, likely cannot turn down a large political contribution from an individual or corporation who may one day ask for a favor in return that might not be in the public's best interest. If the candidate-turned-elected official does what's right and denies their financial supporter, it is reasonable to assume that a political challenger will be recruited to defeat the principled yet "uncooperative" candidate.

All of the above goes on under the radar of the average voter, who is occupied with work, life, family, and friends. A system of public financing, under which candidates for the same offices would have identical resources and no other funding, could go a long way to mitigate an elected official's temptation to act in the interest of a high-dollar donor at the expense of other constituents. In addition, average voters could cast their ballots knowing that their votes were earned by the candidate who best used the very tools that would make a difference once in office, specifically work ethic, creativity, rhetoric, and intellect.

The only way to know who is best prepared for the race of serving in elected office is to create and enforce a quantifiably level playing field that reveals to the public what is on the inside of each person asking for their vote.

Chapter 4

Transportation

A ccess to opportunity can be improved by enhancing the affordability, frequency, and reliability of transportation options for individuals to reach more housing, employment, educational, and recreational choices beyond their current range.

Safely and efficiently moving a society's people and goods is the overarching role of a transportation network. I deeply believe in the value of public transportation, which stems from my own experience as a teenager; when people can reliably and affordably travel to more points within a larger area, there is more just and abundant access to opportunity. In his essay titled *A Testament*

of Hope, posthumously published in January 1969, Dr. Martin Luther King Jr. affirmed that, "Urban transit systems in most American cities, for example, have become a genuine civil rights issue—and a valid one—because the layout of rapid-transit systems determines the accessibility of jobs to the black community." Poor people of all races could begin to improve their lives, King continued, "if transportation systems in American cities could be laid out so as to provide an opportunity for poor people to get meaningful employment."

Multimodal, integrated transit systems are one of my favorite topics. There is enormous value and potential within a publicly accessible network of connected and coordinated transportation options that enable people to step out of their front doors and reach their destinations safely, affordably, and quickly, all while reducing exposure to the risk of error linked to human drivers, traffic congestion, and inclement weather. Expanding public access to safe and reliable transportation options is worth the effort and cost on multiple levels.

Since a life-changing event when I was seventeen years old, public transportation has remained personally important to me. I grew up in the Metropolitan Detroit Area, where one's first words are likely to be "Can I have a ride?" Public transit is limited to a scarcely skeletal bus network, and downtown Detroit's 2.94-mile monorail loop and a street car's initial operating segment of 3.3 miles, which was funded in large part by private donations.

The current transit system is the successor to the robust and extensive streetcar network that served Detroit from the 1860s into the 1950s and the lines of interurban trains that radiated from Detroit toward Port Huron, Flint, Ann Arbor, Toledo, and Ontario, Canada. In fact, between 1890 and 1925, after football games at the University of Michigan, as many as twenty-one interurban cars, the precursor to modern streetcars, handled the crowds from Ann Arbor returning to Detroit.

Prior to Detroit's coronation as the "Paris of the Midwest" in the 1920s and before Henry Ford's assembly line transformed global industry, southeast Michigan had a passenger rail system competitive with New York and Chicago. In the 1830s, the popularity and utility of railroads grew with the rising cost of moving a growing population and its goods by wagon. Woodward Avenue, which in 1818 was authorized by Congress as the country's first paved road for military and postal purposes, determined the route of the Detroit and Pontiac Railroad which began construction in April 1836 and reached approximately twenty-five miles to Pontiac on July 4, 1844; the rail line is still in use today by Amtrak. Transit investment largely peaked shortly after the turn of the twentieth century—not only in Michigan, but nationwide.

In Fall 1995, when my parents sent me to U of D Jesuit, we joined two other families for a carpool to handle the morning and afternoon commute. We'd all meet each morning in the parking lot of a nearby Kroger grocery store and the parent with the assigned day would make the eleven-mile drive to deliver the three seventh-graders before the first bell at 7:45 a.m. While the school required an academic commitment that had never before been asked of me, it called for a logistical commitment that had never been asked of my parents.

The carpool lived on for three years until I made the hockey team and then rode to school with one of my upperclassman teammates. When I turned sixteen during Winter 1999, my parents graciously worked out a deal with my dad's coworker, and, just like that, I had my very own electric blue 1992 Ford Tempo. The car worked out for my parents, too, who were off the hook when I otherwise would have needed a ride that wasn't covered by a fellow student.

A year later, on Valentine's Day of 2000, I was driving home from hockey practice on a standard dark and chilly Michigan winter night. With a tendency to procrastinate that I still haven't fully kicked, I stayed up too late finishing homework that could have been done at a more reasonable hour and started that February 14 as I did most days in high school: on only a few hours of sleep. I was exhausted later in the day on the twenty-five-mile drive from City Ice Arena near the Detroit River to my parents' home in the northwestern suburbs. Since I was used to being tired most evenings, I had come up with a handful of tricks to stay alert just enough to get myself home. I would drive with the car windows open when the outside air was no warmer than 20 degrees Fahrenheit, sing along to any radio station whose songs I knew, which was usually 104.3 WOMC, Detroit's oldies station at the time. I would gulp caffeinated drinks, from coffee to Jolt Cola, and eat Skittles one at a time to stretch out the sugar boost. Despite all of those juvenile tactics to ward off the danger of driving while tired, I was only two miles from home when I could no longer bear the weight of my eyelids. I drifted left of the center line and crashed into two other vehicles. I was snapped awake by the sudden crush of the driver-side door and the shattered driver-side window hitting the left side of my head. With power steering and the brakes both damaged, I struggled to steer to the shoulder and apply the brake pedal with both feet to slow the car enough for the parking brake to be effective on the road's snow-covered gravel shoulder.

The driver-side door was damaged to the point that it lamely clung to the rest of the car like a hangnail. Bypassing the door handle, I unbuckled my seatbelt, pushed open the door, climbed out of the wreckage, and looked at what I had done. Traffic had stopped in both directions as people in the lane nearest me pulled to the shoulder to see if I was okay. The same concern was being shown to the two other drivers whose cars I had hit on the west side of Lahser Road. I walked back to my car and called 911. With the Southfield Police Department en route, I called my mom to let her know why I was not yet home. With the temperature dropping, my car window blown out, and my mom stuck in the traffic jam that I caused, the police officer tending to me kindly offered the backseat of his car so I could step out of the cold. I asked the officer about those in the cars I had hit, and he assured me that they were shaken up but otherwise fine. After a few minutes, my mom pulled up to see her eldest child sitting in the back of a police car with the electric blue Ford Tempo that had been fine earlier that day now rendered undriveable and being towed away.

Knowing the well-deserved reprimand I had coming my way, I sheepishly waved to my mom from the back of the police car. She motioned for me to "get over here," and I had to point to the officer completing the report, since, as I had learned that night, there usually are no door handles in the back of police cars. The officer let me out, and explained to my mom and me how fortunate everyone was that this was a hard side swipe rather than a head-on collision. The officer asked me again if I needed medical attention, which I had initially denied. He took another look at my mom's growing frustration with me and asked if I wanted to reconsider that medical attention.

Growing up, I learned that punishments were like bandages. If you do something wrong, quickly own up to it with an unqualified apology, and ask that the punishment start right away in order to get it over with as soon as possible. The punishment ahead of me that night was like nothing I'd experienced before. With my dad and sisters out of town, my mom had made dinner from scratch for the two of us. Weeknights at home for my family were typically busy. For the most part, we all came home at different times depending on work or practice. It wasn't unusual for my dad to work late; my middle sister swam competitively and often had evening practice; and my mom, after working a full day, would usually help my youngest sister with her homework. With everyone on different schedules, dinner was often up to each person. So for my mom to have gone to the trouble of preparing a meal that was now cold only contributed to my mounting guilt. My mom made me eat that cold food with her as she processed just how close she'd come that night to losing one of her children—not to mention the fact that that child did not fully comprehend the extraordinary fortune of not killing or injuring anyone with such negligent and thoughtless behavior.

To this day, I am grateful that I did not destroy anyone's life on February 14, 2000. Later that same year, I attended a court hearing on the accident. In the courtroom that day was one of the drivers I'd hit. The man made his presence known, and I was given the humbling and invaluable opportunity to hear what he experienced that night and to apologize to his face for my irresponsible behavior and the damage I caused. I do not know that man's name, but I am thankful he took time on a weekday afternoon to put a face on the impact of my negligence.

As a deserved punishment, the court mandated community service and a day-long class for others who'd also driven recklessly. The punishment from my parents was pretty simple: I was grounded until it was consistently warm, which in southeast Michigan was probably early May. They were clever not to define "warm," so the length of my grounding could be extended without violating any of the terms they'd laid out at the start, thus deflating any case I hoped to make for reactivating my social life. Both of my parents worked full-time, so before destroying the car they bought for me, I had been able to help with the logistical burden of shuttling my sisters and myself to our afterschool activities and running occasional errands. Seeing the additional strain I put on my parents to make a trip late on a weekday night in the thick of the school year, a trip I could have taken off their plate before the accident, only added to the festering remorse I felt.

Fast forward seven months to a Fall 2000 meeting at my high school with my parents and my college counselor, Father Ron Torina, SJ. Father Torina was an older Jesuit whose only sign of slowing down was the oxygen tank and attached nasal tube that were always with him. He was razor sharp on the identities and specifics of most of the nation's colleges and universities, and was not encumbered by any sugar-coating when it came to the reasonableness of college options proposed by overly optimistic parents and students.

Let me say that I love my parents dearly, and they love me. However, none of us held any delusions that I was more special than anyone else's child and just needed the right college admission officer to like me and all would be well. That was never anyone's misconception. My parents were rightfully uncompromising on grades and expectations, and because of them, I believe I am in a better position as an adult than I would have been had they gone easy on me and blamed others for my faults and shortcomings.

We walked into our initial college application meeting with Father Torina with that a let's-be-honest and get-to-the-point mentality, which was essential since both my parents were taking time off of work to be there. Immediately realizing that he did not have to massage any inflated perceptions, Father Torina jumped right in with, "Peter, don't name a particular school, but tell me what you want from a college or university."

Growing up in Michigan, you're bound to know people who attended Michigan State University, the University of Michigan, the University of Detroit Mercy, Wayne State University, Western Michigan University, and other great in-state schools that were within a few hours in the car from my parents. However, despite the close proximity to home and the solid reputation of the schools, I was haunted by the thought of driving home for Thanksgiving after little sleep and a full day of class with my eyelids getting heavy, Skittles not doing the trick, and another car accident from which everyone might not walk away.

I responded to Father Torina's question with, "I would prefer to not have to drive between school and my parents' house or at all once I get to school." He nodded and bit his lower lip as he glanced at a framed map of the country on the wall next to his desk, looked at my transcript for a moment, and then started listing schools into three columns: Reach, Reasonable, Safe. Father Torina then asked my parents and me questions about schools we had thought of and why we thought those were potential fits for me and then further pruned his list within the three columns. That conversation ultimately led me to New York City, with its vast public transit network and Fordham University.

Writing for *The New York Times* in September 2012, Sarah Harrison Smith said of the Bronx, home to Fordham University's Rose Hill campus, that "[f]or the students who matriculate here each year, these surroundings might be as much an education as college itself." My four years in the Bronx were indeed an education on every front, particularly when it came to the value of public transportation.

The university's original and primary campus sits on East Fordham Road between multiple subway lines, is about thirty blocks north of Yankee Stadium, and is the namesake for the Metro North commuter railroad station farthest from Grand Central Terminal, which serves both the Harlem and New Haven lines, with the Harlem line heading north into New York's Westchester County and the New Haven line following the northern shore of the Long Island Sound into New Haven, Connecticut, home of the legendary Frank Pepe Pizzeria Napoletana and Yale University. During long weekends and holiday breaks, classmates would head home on the Metro North or take the subway to Penn Station to connect to the Long Island Railroad, New Jersey Transit, or on Amtrak's Northeast Corridor or Keystone Service for anywhere between Washington, DC, Boston, or Harrisburg.

The freedom of not having to ask someone to fight the traffic to pick you up, of not having to rent or borrow a car to go home or to visit someone within the transit foot print, continues to impress and fascinate me. In New York, I was blown away by the interconnected network of tracks, tubes, and tunnels that, when effectively navigated, allowed travelers to remain sheltered from the elements from the point at which they entered the network to where they ultimately exited.

Aside from the ease of efficiently and affordably traveling around a region with which I initially had no familiarity, I found public transit to be a noticeably democratizing force. Ride the downtown-bound #4 subway between 86th Street and Bowling Green on a weekday morning and you could be sandwiched between a panhandler and a multimillionaire. Everyone is on their way, and they are traveling together. Whether you are a busboy or a banker, the shared asset of a functional public transportation network opens doors to opportunities for housing, employment, and recreation that otherwise would be choked off by suffocating automobile traffic or the high cost of owning a car.

The beauty of New York City's transportation system is its connectivity of multiple modes and transit agencies. Land at JFK International Airport, arrive on a train into Grand Central Terminal, or pretty much start from almost any point in the city, and at a relatively inexpensive price, people are afforded equal opportunity to access an almost infinite combination of origin and destination pairs via a series of trains, ferries, and buses. Even more impressive is that many of the transit services are operated independently of each other and coexist in close proximity to form an egalitarian fabric of interwoven transportation options for a sprawling and socioeconomically diverse population.

Affordable access on that scale is a major reason why New York is able to accommodate the population density that contributes to its legendary energy, culture, and productivity. That volume of widespread access should be a prime consideration for other metropolitan areas thoughtfully planning future growth.

In August 2008, my U-Haul and I arrived in Chicago after my now-wife and I agreed that if we wanted to see where a road together could lead, our road would not be starting in New York. We were both from the Midwest and had a network of family and friends in the Chicago area, so I packed up my belongings, took the first accounting job I could get and started learning my beautiful new city.

The growing seriousness of our relationship coupled with boredom at a job that did not address any issues dear to me led to asking myself what was I really interested in and how it could it pay the bills. With my allegiance to the Detroit Lions carrying negative value in Chicago, I began learning everything I could about career options in the transportation industry, a field in which Chicago just happens to be one of the country's hubs.

I engaged experts in conversation during a number of informational interviews and learned a great deal from people at Amtrak, BNSF Railways, The Chicago Transit Authority, The Illinois Department of Transportation, Pace Suburban Bus Service, and a few transportation consulting firms. During those interviews, the interviewees gave generously of their time and perspective. It was over the course of those conversations and my own soul-searching that I refined my area of focus within the field of transportation to passenger rail.

Knowing nothing beyond the experience of occasionally taking a train, I needed to find a path for an accountant to secure a career in passenger rail.

My education had brought me this far, so I figured that more education could take me where I wanted to go next.

Not wanting to leave Chicago, I searched for graduate programs in transportation at schools accessible by public transit, since I did not have nor want a car. Northwestern University in Evanston, just north of Chicago, happened to offer a Master's of Science in Civil Engineering with a focus on Transportation Systems Analysis & Planning. I entered the program and dove into my coursework, learning a great deal about modes of transportation beyond passenger rail.

While completing my thriller of a graduate thesis, *Funding and Sustaining Commuter Rail in Michigan*, I dusted off the practice of reaching out for informational interviews in my quest for a job. I was fortunate to land several interviews that, unfortunately, led to "Thank you, but we've decided to go in another direction." It wasn't until I was on tiny Mackinac Island, between Michigan's lower and upper peninsulas, for a cousin's wedding that fortune struck. I received a phone call with a job offer from Amtrak's office in Oakland, California. Mackinac Island is less than four square miles and does not permit any nonemergency automobiles on the island's roads. Depending on the season, transportation is by foot, bicycle, horse, or snowmobile. I couldn't help but think that maybe being in a place known for embracing alternate forms of transportation had brought luck to someone who firmly believed in options beyond the car. Whether it was my time on Mackinac Island or the fact that two other applicants had turned down the job before it was offered to me, I ecstatically accepted the offer from the National Railroad Passenger Corporation, better known as Amtrak.

Railroads helped build and populate the United States. From the revolutionary passenger services of the New York Central Railroad, Pennsylvania Railroad, and the Baltimore & Ohio Railroad to the transcontinental railroad that was completed when the golden spike was driven at the connection of the Union Pacific and Central Pacific railroads on May 10, 1869, at Promontory Summit in what would eventually become the State of Utah, trains that allowed people and goods to travel vast distances in relatively brief periods of time revolutionized the growth and maturation of our country. Even our modern financial markets were initially shaped by railroads: with capital available once the debt incurred by the War of 1812 was paid off, foreign money began to invest in American railroads. By the 1830s, stock in New Jersey's Camden and Amboy Railroad was available on the London Stock Exchange, and throughout the remainder of the nineteenth century, railroads continued to influence the American landscape and economy through expansion, reorganizations, and mergers. The Pennsylvania Railroad eventually became the world's largest publicly-traded company for a time.

So powerful were railroads that Congress created the Interstate Commerce Commission with the passage of the Interstate Commerce Act of 1887. With many areas wholly reliant on a single railroad for connectivity to markets, medical care, and the rest of the country, the ICC was empowered with regulatory authority to ensure fair rates and access to service. Endowed with immense power, the ICC was the first independent federal agency to operate outside of the departments headed by the president's cabinet and independent of presidential control.

Everything changed on June 21, 1970, when The Pennsylvania Central Transportation Company (Penn Central), the product of the Pennsylvania and New York Central railroads merging in 1968, filed for bankruptcy. The largest bankruptcy in American history at the time, Penn Central was crushed under the weight of accumulating regulations enacted by the ICC, competition from the federally supported Interstate Highway System, and federal routes awarded to airlines before 1978's Airline Deregulation Act. At the time of Penn Central's bankruptcy, the railroad owned and operated the crucial Northeast Corridor, which still runs between Boston and Washington, DC, and remains America's busiest intercity passenger rail line. Congress sensed the looming threat to passenger rail in the country's most densely populated region and to other passenger services operated by other railroads that weren't far behind on the track to bankruptcy.

In October 1970, just four months after Penn Central entered bankruptcy, President Nixon signed the Rail Passenger Service Act, which created the National Railroad Passenger Corporation, better known as Amtrak. In exchange for relief from operating intercity passenger trains, the railroads would grant access to their infrastructure, at a discounted rate, to Amtrak, which would receive taxpayer support to continue operating intercity passenger trains.

My time at Amtrak came thirty-nine years after the company opened its doors on May 1, 1971. My affinity for public transit and my belief in the vast opportunities that improved intercity passenger rail* can deliver to people of all socioeconomic backgrounds has never left me.

At Amtrak, I believed I could help move the company toward providing our country with the high-speed intercity passenger rail that other developed countries enjoy. We wouldn't be inventing anything new; rather,

---

* There are numerous kinds of passenger rail. Commuter rail services typically move passengers within a single metropolitan area. Examples of commuter rail are Metra in Chicago, Metrolink in Los Angeles, Sounder in Seattle, and New Jersey Transit, Metro North, and the Long Island Railroad for New York City. Intercity trains, typically operated by Amtrak, commonly connect two or more major metropolitan areas with intermediate stops along the route.

we would be implementing a proven technology that was safe, functional, and operational all over the world. All I needed to do was get on the inside, learn the ropes, work hard, and move the needle. During my tenure with Amtrak, my belief in the benefits that high-speed intercity passenger could bring to my homeland never wavered, but my assumption that the revolutionary service could come from Amtrak alone was corrected.

As a federally chartered corporation, a majority of whose stock is held by the federal government, Amtrak receives both direction and financial support from Congress. Unfortunately, Amtrak's destiny and the hope of transforming the country's transportation landscape for generations to come are constrained by election cycles and the large costs with long timelines that accompany passenger rail projects. Amtrak's most frequent criticism stems from its portrayal as a money-losing service provider, when it should be judged on a combination of metrics that account for safety, reliability, ridership, and financial stewardship.

With intercity passenger rail in America (aka Amtrak) receiving just enough funding to survive, but never enough to reach the post-WWII type of growth that is ongoing elsewhere around the globe, one has to wonder when political courage and foresight will mature to the point of evaluating transportation projects' multigenerational merits on factors such permanent jobs created, constituents served, and, most important, lives in transit saved, rather than just cost recovery.

The Great Fire that devastated Chicago in 1871 remains a pivotal moment in the city's history, enough so as to merit one of the stars on the Chicago city flag that represent four of the city's most significant events (the other three are the Battle of Fort Dearborn in 1812, the World's Columbian Exposition of 1893, and the Century of Progress Exposition of 1933–34). Up from the rubble of the Great Fire rose a new city, a second city, that improved upon the dated layout that was in place up until the blaze. The clean slate, despite its tragic means, afforded Chicago the opportunity to reimagine itself and plan for growth more thoughtfully than could be accomplished through the incremental approach that came with Chicago's development from a frontier settlement to an American metropolis. The second Chicago, the one we know today, is a result of not being bound by the restrictive decisions of a past era.

Seventy-four years after The Great Chicago Fire, Japan was brought to surrender when the atomic bomb was dropped over Hiroshima and Nagasaki, respectively. In the wake of the war's destruction, Japanese officials revived discussion of *Shinkansen*, translated as "bullet train," an idea that initially was proposed in the 1930s. After the war, rail was preferred over air travel for rebuilding Japan in order to avoid the impression that the country might be rearming and because of rail's ability to quickly and reliably move masses of people and goods into and out of heavily congested urban centers and sprawling metropolitan regions where land was and remains at a premium.

Led by three visionaries who had designed Japanese aircraft during the war, Japanese National Railways (JNR) successfully pushed back against a growing animosity towards railroads and preference for air travel and highways that was saturating transportation policy in much of Europe and the United States. At the behest JNR's president, the Japanese government approved the *Shinkansen* project late in 1958, with construction starting the following spring on the country's first segment of high-speed rail between Tokyo and Osaka.

While construction of the first segment was grossly over budget, the line was open for business in time for the 1964 Olympic games in Tokyo. Despite the financial cost, the genie was out of the bottle and customers steadily flocked to the punctuality, convenience, and speed of high-speed rail. High-speed rail is not solely responsible for the vast strides made by Japan in postwar reconstruction, but high-speed rail was then and remains today a vital component of the superpower's infrastructure.

The success and value of high-speed rail should be measured by nonfinancial metrics as well, such as safety and on-time performance. In fact, since *Shinkansen* service commenced in 1964, there has not been a single reported injury or fatality to a passenger on board a single one of the high-speed trains. Trains operate on schedule with an annual average delay of less than sixty seconds, which includes delays caused by natural disasters and other uncontrollable factors. In fact, the management of a train line that serves Tokyo actually issued an official apology when, on November 14, 2017, one of its trains departed the station twenty seconds *ahead* of schedule. With that level of pride and commitment to performance, it is no wonder that Japanese passenger rail is among the world's gold standards of public transportation. There is no reason Americans should not want the same for our own transportation network.

One of the neatest design features of *Shinkansen* is the front of those train sets that resemble a duck's bill. The story goes that due to the high speeds at which *Shinkansen* was changing atmospheric conditions from the open air of the countryside to the nearby walls of a precisely built tunnel, an engineer began looking at design changes to minimize the loud and disruptive boom from the other end of the tunnel that came with the train hitting the air confined within the tunnel, similar to the piston in an internal combustion engine. The engineer realized that with the duckbill, nature had long ago perfected the design that would address *Shinkansen*'s problem. For ducks flying above the water in search of fish and then diving in at a high rate of speed, the bill displaces water as the rest of the duck's body smoothly cuts through the water faster than the targeted fish can escape. Who would have thought that waterfowl could unlock the design solution for a precise and highly complex passenger rail system? Often, we just need to look at something with a fresh set of eyes and an open mind to entice innovative answers to reveal themselves in unlikely places.

Those presently in and seeking leadership roles must prune away obstructions to progress, rather than wait for a "great fire" to provide opportunities to reimagine the future. We should gratefully stand on the knowledge revealed by those before us as we pursue the modernization of our infrastructure on the scale of Chicago after The Great Fire and Japan after WWII. Tragedy is not necessary to breed opportunity, nor is the absence of tragedy an acceptable excuse to remain apathetic to practices and policies that have overstayed their useful lives.

❧

Transportation policy affects us all. Everything we consume or use must get to us somehow. For service providers, manufacturers, employees, and individuals, our transportation networks and the policies that have shaped them to this point will guide future decisions and will remain crucial to all of us who depend on those networks and to the people who build and maintain them. In fact, the public transportation industry alone directly employs about 400,000 individuals, and for each $1 billion invested in public transportation, 50,700 jobs are created and supported, according to 2013 estimates from the American Public Transportation Association (APTA).

Infrastructure cannot be outsourced. Buy America provisions in many publicly funded projects support the procurement of American-made materials, but even if a component is foreign sourced, the end result is assembled on American soil. Once built, construction and engineering workers can move on to the next project while the final product is operated and maintained by skilled workers. In addition to creating jobs, public transportation brings employees to and from work. According to the APTA, of 2013's 10.7 billion trips on public transit, nearly 60 percent were work commutes.

America's last major transportation infrastructure project constructed new roads of access to opportunity. Acknowledged as such by the U.S. Department of Commerce, the National System of Interstate and Defense Highways was, according to the Bureau of Public Roads, "the greatest peacetime public works program in history." Initiated by President Wilson's signing of the Federal Aid Road Act of 1916 and advanced by President Franklin Roosevelt's delivery of a hand-drawn map of eight superhighways to the chief of the Bureau of Public Roads, the interstate highway system was carried over the goal line by President Eisenhower, who came to support the system after driving the German Autobahn during World War II. The autobahn provided then-General Eisenhower a lens through which to see a large-scale transportation infrastructure project as a component of national defense. The American interstate system officially launched with the National Interstate and Defense Highways Act of 1956.

For many Americans, such as myself, the interstate system, like air conditioning or microwave ovens, has always existed during our lifetime. The same applies to much of our country's aging, yet crucial, transportation infrastructure. We rely on our infrastructure without respecting our future dependence enough to adequately invest in the maintenance and modernization of our roads, bridges, tracks, tunnels, sewers, power grid and more. Infrastructure projects are expensive. If well-planned and executed, the projects, once built, are often valued more by the public for their utility than they are criticized for their staggering price tags. When we drive on an interstate highway, we don't comment on the cost per mile to build the road. If anything, we complain about congestion or the condition of the road, rather than the interstate's financial performance. Taxpayers are not inherently opposed to large infrastructure projects or improved transportation options, but they are understandably wary of funding projects plagued with missed deadlines, red tape, corruption, and waste.

For a national project as big as high-speed rail to leave the station, steps must first be taken to improve taxpayer confidence that, at the very minimum, fair value will be returned for every public dollar spent and that the costs, whether budgeted or unforeseen, will be proactively disclosed to taxpayers. The first step to building an infrastructure project whose scale would rival the Interstate Highway System is building trust with taxpayers through an innovative and informative real-time reporting system that will provide peace of mind during planning and construction to taxpayers who are concerned their money is being wasted.

As mentioned earlier, no one likes a bill of any sort, but if you feel that you are not being ripped off, that you are actually receiving adequate value for your money, well, that is solid ground on which to start every conversation on publicly-funded projects. The thing is, people are not usually upset when their tax dollars support something they support. Take the interstate highway system, whose construction and maintenance costs do not frequently come up on the evening news or among most taxpayers. After all, when was the last time you heard someone ask, "Can you believe how much it cost to build I-90?" Of course not, because what would we do without it?

We will never be able to build enough capacity on our roads to completely alleviate automobile congestion, so the next step is high-speed rail similar to the systems currently operating in China, Japan, and western Europe. Compared to highways, high-speed rail consumes less real estate, has a faster running time, is less susceptible to our increasingly volatile and changing climate, has greater on-time performance compared to road and air travel, and, with sufficient frequency, allows people to comfortably adjust their schedules with flexibility that is competitive with a personal automobile.

High-speed rail will not be cheap, and will take longer than a single election cycle to build. The benefits of high-speed rail will be realized only with incremental progress, great financial cost, and courageous elected officials who might be unlikely to reap the political rewards that would come when constituents finally realize the benefits of high-speed rail. However, looking only as far as the next election is regrettably shortsighted and punts the issue to our children and grandchildren, the same children and grandkids in whose interest so many elected officials love to say they're working. Today's elected officials should strive for a legacy that is more than just the number of terms accumulated by supporting laws and programs that likely will not materialize in time to benefit their political or actual lives. True high-speed rail in America is one of those programs on which a lasting legacy can be built.

Former Vice President Joe Biden is a plainspoken and gifted politician with a magnetic presence tailormade for elected office. Biden, Delaware's favorite son, might have cut short his career in public service after an unthinkable personal tragedy, if not for the access to opportunity afforded by Amtrak's Northeast Corridor.

In 1972, at the age of 29, Joe Biden was a husband, father of three young children and a member of the New Castle County Council when he won a stunning upset over an entrenched incumbent to represent the State of Delaware in the U.S. Senate. A little over a month after his electoral victory, his 30-year-old wife and 1-year-old daughter were killed in a car accident that also left his sons, ages 3 and 4, respectively, both hospitalized. In the wake of devastation, Biden was able to fulfill the instinctive desire of a parent to be physically present for his surviving children and take his seat in the Senate because Amtrak's high level of service between Washington, D.C. and Wilmington, Delaware allowed him to easily and reliably make the 259-mile daily round trip from his home to Capitol Hill.

The people of the United States are a beneficiary of Joe Biden's long tenure of progressive and bold service as both a Senator and Vice President. Joe Biden ended up as a beneficiary of the investment that was made by the Pennsylvania Railroad generations before. Amtrak carries on the legacy of intercity passenger rail along the Northeast corridor, and continues to provide travelers between Washington and Boston with an option that is often superior to traveling by air or car.

A sustained and significant commitment at the local, state, and federal level to the planning and construction of modern and expansive public transportation will benefit every age and socioeconomic group, and improve the odds that talent will be better able to access a wider horizon of employment, housing, educational, treatment and recreational opportunity—even when that opportunity means a 259-mile daily commute. As Joe Biden's time between Wilmington and Washington proved and American author Paul Theroux once said, "Anything is possible on a train."

Chapter 5

A Nation of Where Are You From

A ccess to opportunity can be improved by minimizing obstacles that discourage and delay the contributions of the brightest and hardest-working immigrants who are willing to leave their home country for the United States. Attracting and embracing good, hardworking people to the American population is an opportunity we as a nation cannot forsake or take for granted. There is no guarantee that any country will permanently remain a desirable destination for immigrants, therefore steps should be taken to ensure *that our homeland remains attractive and welcoming to the best of humanity, both within and beyond our borders.*

Like most Americans, I grew up with the question "Where are you from?" When "Michigan" or "the Detroit Area" wasn't the answer the questioner wanted, the question was rephrased along the lines of where my ancestors originated or, "No, where are you from-from?" As for my background, I am French, Irish, German, and Hungarian. My last name is of French origin and, according to Google, means, "one who lives by the roses."

At what point do we stop asking each other where we're from and just say that we're all Americans? I don't know the circumstances under which my ancestors came to the United States, but I am far more concerned that our nation could eventually deny entry and accommodation to the next generation of tired, poor, huddled masses who are irreplaceable assets in every chapter of the American story. This begs the question of which future superpower would welcome those in search of refuge and will benefit from the culture, experience, and work ethic that they add to a society. As a nation, we cannot simultaneously lead the world and isolate ourselves from it. Bad people can come from anywhere, and while as a country we must always remain vigilant, we must not succumb to the laziness of prejudice.

Our country, our union of states is more than lines on a map, words on a document, or colors on a flag. The simplest and most desirable ideas, if given the courage to be enacted, can yield the most profound results. Take the idea to reject tyranny, tribalism, and ethnic preference, and open a country's doors to citizens of the planet who want something more for what they personally hold dear: to live without fear of persecution for practicing one's religious beliefs that do not infringe upon the rights of another and for their children to receive a quality education in an environment of open-mindedness and growth, rather than indoctrination. Our country is a laboratory of means to access opportunity, with new avenues emerging (although under threat from those who want America to look, think and pray a certain way).

As someone born into the bounty and rights afforded to citizens of the United States, I'll never fully appreciate what America means to those who intentionally earned their citizenship. Doing my best to empathize, I imagine my homeland being a refuge of safety from civil unrest, military rule, tyranny, famine, and other hazards of daily life in many parts of the world.

❦

Rajesh Chandrakant Vora (best known as Raj) and I first met after attending the same wedding at St. Mary of the Angels church in Chicago's Bucktown neighborhood. After the ceremony, the wedding party took photos around downtown Chicago while the rest of us killed time at Cortland's Garage, a bar walking distance from the church, until it was time for the reception. At the bar, Raj and I introduced ourselves and realized that we had a number of things in common, among them our shared profession of accounting.

Raj moved to the United States from Ahmedabad (pronounced Om-Duh-Bod), India, in September 1981 and was married to his wife, Arti, earlier that year. Initially arriving in New Jersey, they moved to St. Louis, where Raj's older brother was a professor of biology at St. Louis University. In India, Raj was licensed as a Chartered Accountant, the equivalent of a CPA in America. However, without a similar Memorandum of Understanding like the one between India and Britain for Chartered Accountants, Raj was without the qualification that had been his livelihood. No matter. Raj got himself a job as a staff accountant for a local CPA and began preparing for the CPA exam, while his wife, Arti, worked in the biology lab of Washington University and they prepared for the arrival of their first child.

After eight years of working for someone else, Raj picked up a steadily growing amount of tax and accounting work, which he did from his kitchen table on nights and weekends as a licensed CPA in his own right. Once it became apparent that the trajectory of his side business's workload would continue upward,

Raj made the exhilarating decision to hang out his shingle and open his own practice. While Raj was an exceptionally competent accountant with an encyclopedic knowledge and sincere appreciation for the tax code, it was his soft skills that set him apart.

While Raj was a CPA by training, he also was a sympathetic ear and trusted advisor to friends and clients on matters ranging from buying a home, navigating the immigration process, working with family members as business partners, and bringing up children in a culture with traditions and accepted practices different from the ones the parents knew. Although Raj was not perfect himself, for those in need of assistance, or at the very least, empathy, he was just right.

Regardless of whether someone was applying for their green card or their ancestors had come over on the Mayflower, Raj could be counted on to listen happily and reply honestly. If he could help, he would say so. If the issue was outside of his expertise, he'd give his best referral. If the distressed person just needed a sounding board, well, that was fine, too. With a sincere focus on the client as a person and a commitment to providing exceptional service, Raj built a CPA firm that thrives today with offices in St. Louis and Chicago.

Over the years, I've known Raj to be twice as smart as me, have twice the personality—and be twice as susceptible to distraction. (He can't be better than me at everything.) We remain close, and I continue to learn so much from him, as he possesses a perspective I can only see from the outside: that of an immigrant to the United States.

I love my country and am eternally grateful to have been born here. And while it was not my decision where to be born, it is my decision to stay; an experience far removed from leaving one's native homeland, culture, language, family, and more to pursue a life in America against obstacles that most natural-born citizens will never know exist. I admire Raj and others like him, people who saw what they wanted in the United States and took the risks, made the sacrifices, and put in the work to make America happen for them.

Raj has benefited from the access to opportunity found in America. Likewise, America is richer because of Raj and people like him. He is a person whose success has affected everyone in his life, except for himself.

I know these things about Raj Vora because he is my father-in-law. Since that first conversation after the 2008 wedding in Chicago where my now-wife was in the wedding party that was off taking photos, Raj and I have grown close as friends and on October 20, 2012, we officially became family.

Growing up, my parents never gave me a talk about the birds and the bees. My dad assumed that was the responsibility of biology class, and my mom, who was a bit more willing to broach more mature topics, limited her advice to "You don't just marry the person, you marry their family." As a middle-schooler, my mom's advice was given far too early for it to be practical, yet it remains some of the best advice I've ever received. I am so lucky to have married not only into a family of good and kind people, but into a group of individuals who've expanded my horizons and exposed me to issues I'll never fully understand but am better for knowing they exist.

By the time I met Raj, his CPA practice was an established success. It was through meeting many of his clients and learning the stories through the eyes of those who sought his guidance on matters of accounting, taxes, and the nuances of making one's way in America that I saw what his journey might have been like. It was through those stories and encounters that I learned a new angle of empathy: to appreciate an experience without possessing it.

I'll never truly experience the struggles, smirks, and stereotypes an immigrant is likely to face. Such an inability to fully relate is simply more reason to take advantage of every opportunity to learn from those who know first-hand what it feels like to come from another country and try to make it in America. The growth of our country's population, culture, society, and innovation know-how should continue through a balance of procreation, adoption, and immigration, just as it always has. American-born children, those adopted by loving parents, and those who immigrated are all essential our nation's economic and cultural force that is capable of becoming increasingly formidable with the growing influx of talent and diversity brought by each successive generation.

It is not an exaggeration to state that, without immigration, I would not have the two best parts of my life: my wife and daughter. I dated other people before meeting my wife, but I have never met anyone who can compare to her. Her parents, their culture, and her experiences growing up are part of the person I fell in love with. We now intentionally share much of the same culture that was present in my wife's childhood with our daughter, who, hopefully, will benefit from the exposure to traditions and values that her grandparents brought with them from the other side of the world.

◈

During his run for Governor of Illinois in September 2017, I heard Chris Kennedy, nephew of our 35th president, speak in the back room of Chief O'Neill's Pub & Restaurant on Elston Avenue in Chicago. In his stump speech, Kennedy pointed out something about Chicago's citywide enjoyment and enrichment, which stems from the numerous cultures that thrive within the Windy City. Chicago is not perfect, and it remains heavily segregated, but, as Kennedy highlighted, we are a city that enjoys each other's food, celebrates each other's culture, enjoys traditions for religious holidays we may not observe, and intermarries and makes homes that preserve multicultural traditions. We learn from each other to create new options never before experienced, such as the fusion of different culinary traditions into a singular cuisine. In many ways the appropriation of another culture demonstrates appreciation too.

By opening your palate, your mind, and your heart to people beyond what's familiar, you can find a new favorite dish or discover an artist whose work strikes a chord, or even learn a new word from a different language that conveys a feeling more aptly than your native tongue. Our nation has done the work of attracting bright and hardworking people who have knowledge and perspective informed by circumstances many of us will never fully appreciate. Our fellow countrymen of ethnic backgrounds different than our own are walking encyclopedias of humanity and assets to the American experience who deserve respect.

∽

My mother-in-law, Arti Vora, was born in New York City while her father, Dr. V.C. Shah, completed postdoctoral work at Columbia University. During those years, Arti was a regular kid living in Manhattan. In the Upper West Side walk-up where her family lived, she'd climb the stairs to play at her friend's apartment, whose family had also emigrated to the United States.

During a visit home to India, Arti's pregnant mother gave birth to a second child, a little girl. Already struggling to get by in New York on the little money they had, my wife's grandparents made the gut-wrenching decision to leave their infant daughter with family in India while they returned to America to access the postdoctoral opportunity available to her father. Five years later, Arti and her parents returned to India for good. There is a priceless photo of Arti and her sister meeting for what must have felt like the first time, Arti in clothes common for a little American girl and her sister in clothes typical for a little girl in India.

Dr. Shah, my wife's grandfather, went on to lecture around the world and conduct renowned research from his home base at the Indian Institute of Management in Ahmedabad. Who knows if his ability to provide for his family and the impact of his research would have been compromised had he not completed his postdoctoral work at Columbia. However hard the decision must have been, he and his wife made what was the best decision at the time for their family. I am grateful for every decision that ultimately led to me becoming a member of their family, particularly the decision to initially come to New York that resulted in my mother-in-law being born an American citizen, which smoothed the path for her and my father-in-law to settle in the U.S.

After their marriage in 1981, Raj and Arti left India to start their new life together in the United States. Another timeless photo shows the entire extended family seeing them off at the gate of their Air India flight from New Delhi to Newark. Despite comfort from loved ones in close proximity in their new home in St. Louis, there were moments of fear and isolation that come with any new situation, although amplified by the abrupt changes in climate and culture.

My in-laws did not know the challenges they'd face assimilating to life in a country and culture very different from the one they left, but they leaned on their promise to each other and focused on the life they wanted for their family as they undertook the hard work and sacrifice that would bring them the prosperity they've built today.

As a graduate student from 2009–10, I shared an office space with students from Northwestern University's Center for Advanced Cement-Based Materials. (Yes, it was a center focused entirely on cement.) Of my four officemates, all of whom couldn't have been nicer, one was a lady visiting from eastern Europe who changed my perspective on cement. She mentioned that her home country lacked many of the natural resources for construction that other countries enjoy, so builders in her homeland used various forms of cement as a primary building material. She explained that different components in a cement mixture can perform differently in different environments.

In July 2017, *Time* magazine featured an article about a research paper that had been published in *American Mineralogist*. The research found that the durability of two-thousand-year-old Roman seawalls originated in what was a newly discovered chemical reaction. Modern cement mixtures typically erode over time when exposed to saltwater. But the ancient Romans' mixture of volcanic ash, lime, and a mineral called aluminium tobermorite became stronger in the presence of seawater, enough so that the integrity of the seawalls have remained intact since they were built around the time of Christ.

The study's lead author, Marie Jackson of the University of Utah, said that "[c]ontrary to the principles of modern cement-based concrete, the Romans created a rock-like concrete that thrives in open chemical exchange with seawater." It is the coexistence with thousands of years of relentless waves that led to the mixture of lime and silica oxides blooming within the volcanic rock aggregate and mortar that produced a cement that grows stronger to this day.

The whole point to my cement story is that ingredients, which otherwise would not benefit each other, can form a strong bond that serves the greater good and strengthens with age when placed in the right location. It is no coincidence that fallen empires are typically built from homogenous societies. This is why the recurring diversity of America's population is not only what helped build the country, but remains key to its continued prosperity.

Whether it is an advance in cement-based materials or maintaining status as a world power, success is not realized by simply copying a recipe. With regard to the Roman cement, Marie Jackson mentioned that the "Romans were fortunate in the type of rock they had to work with. They observed that volcanic ash grew cements to produce the [mortar]. We don't have those rocks in a lot of the world, so there would have to be substitutions made." Likewise, America's recipe for success is no secret, but it has not been replicated elsewhere because all the components must be just right for something special and lasting to grow. Our land, our laws, our long-standing embrace of immigrants must all remain firmly grounded and upright for America's best hope of avoiding the fate of humanity's vanished empires.

As American citizens, we must welcome, embrace, and advance immigrants without regard to ethnicity, income, religion, or whom one loves. Like the waves that simultaneously battered and fortified the Roman seawalls, our nation can continue to grow stronger only by embracing all talent and promise, whether homegrown or imported.

Chapter 6

Civic Engagement for an Arriving Generation

∾

*A*ccess to opportunity can be improved by pursuing *leadership roles that can support the values each generation wants to advance in their finite time at society's helm.*

∾

President Obama compared civic leadership to a relay race. A successful relay team depends on a smooth baton transfer when the runner handing off is nearing the end of his or her top speed and the runner receiving the baton is approaching his or her peak, with the baton always moving to a fresher and more energized runner. As my generation of Millennials grips the baton and proceeds forward as earnestly as the generations before us, we must remember the importance of our responsibility to groom the next generation for the roles of civic leadership in which our temporary tenure is just now beginning.

Our generation can do better than previous ones not because we are better, but because we have more: more resources, more access to information, and more awareness of social issues, and thus more of an obligation to carry the baton farther than those before us. Doing our best with everything available is not only what Millennials owe to ourselves, but also what we owe to the generations that set the table for us and those for whom we're obligated to leave it set better than it was for us. I hope to be part of a generational legacy that is greater and more lasting than thinking only of our own comfort and leaving subsequent generations to solve the most threatening and vexing challenges that we did not have the courage to approach.

I am not afraid of losing my current race, which should not be mistaken as overconfidence in my chances of winning, but I am terrified of not consistently performing to the upper limits of my courage and ability should I win. All levels of the political landscape are littered with elected officials who thought they would be in office long enough to patiently address their constituents' most pressing issues, those who became complacent because the office felt like it was theirs for as long as they wanted, and those elected on the promise to produce something great, only to squander their opportunity in exchange for petty political points.

Near the University of Chicago, at the western end of a grassy stretch, called the Midway Plaisance, there is an imposing sculpture titled *Fountain of Time*. Unveiled in 1920, it is a unique perspective of Time standing still as generations of humanity pass before it. This thought-provoking sculpture is a reminder that every generation is operating on a limited time, affixed to an unstoppable and finite conveyer. For those in elected office, no matter the polling numbers, the balance in the campaign account, or number of electoral wins, when your last day arrives, whether in office or on this Earth, will you be proud of how you handled your opportunity to help those who needed help? Will you look in the mirror and see someone who did more to improve the lives of the most vulnerable in our society than you did to fulfill your own personal ambition?

Civic Engagement

Becoming civically engaged is a form of service to your community, your government, your household, and your priorities. As articulated by French philosopher and fellow Jesuit student Joseph de Maistre centuries ago, "In a democracy people get the leaders they deserve." You can support or become the leader that your community needs to reach the greatness it deserves.

In 2014, my wife and I moved back to Chicago, and that October, I read an article that changed my point of view on how to engage in the West Town neighborhood where we had bought our first home. The article was about a conversation that the area's congressman, Representative Mike Quigley of Illinois' Fifth Congressional district, had with the DePaul University Democrats. During his conversation with the students, Congressman Quigley said something that struck me, and which I still regard as clear and timeless advice for anyone thinking of public service. He said, "All the time I have people who come up to me who don't understand this, I ask them, 'Have you ever been to a community meeting? Have you ever worked on a school board issue? A library board?'"

I asked myself the congressman's questions, and soon after joined my neighborhood association and became a volunteer commissioner of my local Special Service Area, which applies taxpayer dollars to enhance the area's commercial corridors beyond what is provided by city services. By getting involved within the existing civic organizations closest to my home, I developed a deep appreciation for my neighbors and my neighborhood's history, all of which are key components of civic engagement.

As James Madison wrote in Federalist No. 62:

> It is not possible that an assembly of men called for the most part from pursuits of a private nature, continued in appointment for a short time, and led by no permanent motive to devote intervals of public occupation to a study of the laws, the affairs, and the comprehensive interests of their country, should, if left wholly to themselves, escape a variety of important errors in the exercise of their legislative trust.

In other words, those who make our laws are fallible, and so the laws they pass can be, too. As humans, we can stubbornly stick by our mistakes to our own detriment, but the public cannot afford elected officials who indulge pride or ignorance. To remedy poorly written laws and outdated or unjust practices, new blood that has not been infected by indebtedness to the old ways must be regularly injected into public office to keep fresh the pursuit of more equitable access to opportunity for a perpetually changing population.

The United States is not and was never meant to be an effortlessly sustainable experiment in evolving self-governance; your contribution of respectful involvement is essential. Said more effectively than I ever could, is a scene from Aaron Sorkin's *The American President*, in which the president passionately states that:

> America isn't easy. America is advanced citizenship. You've gotta want it bad, 'cause it's gonna put up a fight. It's gonna say, 'You want free speech? Let's see you acknowledge a man whose words make your blood boil, who's standing center stage and advocating at the top of his lungs that which you would spend a lifetime opposing at the top of yours.' You want to claim this land as the land of the free? Then the symbol of your country cannot just be a flag. The symbol also has to be one of its citizens exercising his right to burn that flag in protest. Now show me that, defend that, celebrate that in your classrooms. Then, you can stand up and sing about the land of the free.

❧

In his first public event since leaving The White House, President Obama publicly reflected on his own political journey during an April 2017 conversation at his former employer, the University of Chicago. In the midst of writing his presidential memoir, President Obama recommended to the audience not to do something just because it's the next step, which he credited as a major reason for his failed 1998 campaign for Illinois' 1st Congressional district. He also said that the key tenet for those interested in public service is to "[w]orry less about what you want to be, and worry more about what you want to do."

David Axelrod, President Obama's former political advisor, remains a storied fixture within Chicago's political habitat. Prior to his days in The White House, Axelrod was a sought-after consultant for hungry Democratic candidates. In his 2015 memoir, *Believer: My Forty Years in Politics*, Axelrod recounted cautionary examples of hollow candidates driven by fame and ambition rather than a desire to selflessly serve their constituents.

As a thirteen-year-old on the Lower East Side of Manhattan, Axelrod worked for three dollars an hour distributing literature for a New York State Assembly candidate whose father was bankrolling the campaign to buy his son a win in what became the state assembly's most expensive campaign at the time. When Axelrod's employer won on election night, the thirteen-year-old was left with the lasting memory of accepting money to "install an unworthy nitwit in public office."

Years later, as a professional political consultant, Axelrod was contacted by a Chicago congressman with whom he had a previous working relationship and who was planning a run for governor of Illinois. That congressman's name was Rod Blagojevich. When Axelrod asked why he wanted to be governor, Blagojevich replied "You can help me figure that out." Axelrod passed up working on Blagojevich's 2002 gubernatorial campaign in accordance with the same principle President Obama would articulate fifteen years later for those interested in public service.

No political party is perfect. The platforms of both the Democratic and Republican parties represent the priorities and positions of large blocs of American citizens. I am a Democrat not because I dislike Republicans, but because I deeply believe that progressive-leaning policies, while not perfect, can facilitate more just access to opportunity for all people, particularly those who are at greater risk of being underrepresented, underresourced and vulnerable to poverty. Despite identifying as a Democrat, I believe that having two stable and well-informed major political parties is healthy at the local, state, and national levels. The rot of either party creates a vacuum filled by hot tempers, hollow candidates, and fringe positions.

Even if Democrats were elected in every office at every level of government, problems such as hot tempers, hollow candidates, and fringe positions on the left side of the aisle would still bubble. The same goes triple for Republicans (just kidding!) America's citizens, businesses and allies are all best served when the United States is guided and driven by constructive, fact-based, and respectful political discourse.

It is in the mutual interest of voters and political parties to always be cultivating deep benches of qualified and prepared candidates who can begin developing policies and solutions with future generations in mind, rather than just the next election cycle. Put simply, the occupant of an office should not be the only one thinking about how to improve that office. In the words of Oliver Wendell Holmes, Sr.: "Many ideas grow better when transplanted into another mind than in the one where they sprang up." Indeed, an idea rarely explores all avenues of its potential in the mind where it originated, so it is imperative to constantly seek inspiration and run as far as you can with it. Great ideas are all around us, and they are just waiting for someone to make them better with his or her own perspective and by connecting them to other great ideas.

A Useful Cliff

An idea which I've come to think of as "A Useful Cliff" originally came from legendary investor Warren Buffet. A *usual* cliff is useless; it is something you can fall down or something that you can be pushed toward as a threat. However, a useful cliff is a way of pushing to the limit whomever you want to make perform; in this case, elected officials.

During a July 2011 interview with CNBC during the midst of a federal budget standoff, Warren Buffett proposed a specific cliff should Congress not pass an adequate budget, noting that, "I could end the deficit in five minutes. You just pass a law that says that any time there's a deficit of more than three percent of GDP, all sitting members of Congress are ineligible for reelection. Yeah, yeah, now you've got the incentives in the right place, right?"

The incentive to dig in one's heels to appease or energize a political base and decrease the odds of a primary challenge is appealing for many elected officials, both within and beyond the State of Illinois. If only there were a worthwhile reward for working together, and a swift statutory purge for obstructionism.

In the spirit of Buffett's original idea, I would suggest that a legislative body and the accompanying executive, such as a city council and a mayor, a state assembly and a governor, or Congress and the president, should be required to pass and sign into law a balanced budget, covering no less than twelve months, no later than 11:59 p.m. on the day before the existing budget expires. By doing so, every member of the legislature and the executive would remain eligible for reelection in the next election cycle, unless term limits are already in force. Should the deadline not be met, for any reason whatsoever, the legislature and the executive collectively would be ineligible for reelection in the subsequent cycle.

Many elected officials have long been motivated by self-preservation. It's time for constituents and municipalities to benefit from the desire for self-preservation that burns within our politicians. Progress requires pressure. It is time for those we've elected to operate under an ultimatum to work together and produce, at the very least, a balanced budget at least once a year, or take a break from their office, even if only for a term.

For individuals, nonprofits, and businesses that suffer from partisan gridlock that delays or prevents a dependable long-term budget commitment from their respective layers of government, just imagine the benefits if our elected officials were motivated by a factor as compelling as the prospect of reelection hinging on the ability to pass a budget every year by a deadline on which every town, city, county, school board, police department, and taxpayer could rely. Should a legislator or executive believe they are faced with choosing between compromise or conscience, each should operate under the knowledge that if the deadline for a balanced budget is not met because of their vote or veto, they and every member of both parties will take a seat for at least one cycle. After all, the commitment to your values is only as real as the consequences you are willing to face.

As Supreme Court Justice Ruth Bader Ginsburg once put it, "Collegiality is crucial to the success of our mission." Legislators and executives at every level of government are a team and to compromise is not to surrender. Their primary function is to work together in the interest of their constituents. If they cannot or will not work together, it is simply time to pick a new team. While some good lawmakers might be unable to run for reelection, if they are that good, they'll have a strong and defensible record on which to run should they want to reclaim their seat. Performance mandates are the answer for legislative productivity. Term limits are not. Should your unit of government be fortunate enough to have a legislative body and executive that work together, let them continue to produce until they insist upon no longer collaborating, and then clear the roster and start anew. I would rather have too little of a promising option, than too much of one that offers nothing more.

The thought of losing my race has become my useful cliff. I think of having to deliver a concession speech while asking myself "What could I have done differently?" By pushing myself to imagine defeat, I hope to see the landscape of my current race and my own shortcomings as a candidate more objectively so that my campaign can benefit from helpful perspectives that otherwise might not arrive until after the March 20, 2018, Democratic primary. Hopefully embracing a measure of productive discomfort will help make me the best candidate I can be at every opportunity I'm given.

The Office Belongs to the People

As citizens, we should seek to extract maximum value, not longevity, from our elected officials. By affording elected officials the perception of unlimited time in office, we give politicians license to procrastinate on enacting initiatives or legislation that is in the public's best interest but might not be politically convenient at the time.

The idea of a legislator passing legislation that increases the risk of him or her not being reelected is far-fetched. Why would a legislator act against his or her own self-interest, even though it is in the interest of their constituents? Most elected officials initially stepped into politics with the best of intentions, yet at a certain point, self-preservation puts improving the odds of reelection above the assumed desire to enact positive change that originally drew each individual into his or her first race. An elected official should always feel a sense of pride for their office, but never ownership. With a sense of ownership comes a shift in focus from faithfully executing the office in question to worrying more about fortifying the defenses of one's political turf, which detracts from focusing on those whom the office exists to serve.

Long before Warren Buffett suggested his cure for gridlock among American politicians, Lucius Quinctius Cincinnatus, better known simply as Cincinnatus, personified the ideal public servant. In 460 BC, well before the rise of the Roman Empire, Cincinnatus retired to his modest farm following his service as Roman consul, the Roman republic's highest elected political office. Two years after rejoining his family and his farm, Rome came under threat of invasion by a tribe known as the Aequians. Found plowing his fields, Cincinnatus was approached by members of the Senate and implored to assume dictatorial authority and vanquish the approaching threat. According to legend, Cincinnatus famously set down his plow, donned his old senatorial toga, led the Roman soldiers to a surrender of the Aequians, abdicated his far-reaching authority, and then returned to his farm, all in the span of fifteen days.

More than two millennia later, another brilliant military leader and statesman would be called from his farm, this one in Mount Vernon, Virginia, to lead the Continental Army against the British Empire. In the mold of Cincinnatus, General George Washington answered the call when asked to serve as the first president of a new nation. Despite the ability to retain power indefinitely, President Washington set the precedent for one of our country's greatest traditions, the peaceful transition of power. Relinquishing the presidency, Washington quietly returned to his farm. Labeled by the British poet Lord Byron as "the Cincinnatus of the West," the similarities between Washington and Cincinnatus are striking and perhaps destined, including their mutual embrace of agriculture, which Washington saw as essential for America's hope of economic independence from the British Empire.

By stepping aside for other leaders to take over, both Cincinnatus and Washington induced growth, encouraged the embrace of responsibility, and made room for new ideas and leaders to flourish. Each generation should do likewise when the succeeding generation is hitting their stride.

Elected office should never descend into a static career of continuous self-preservation. It should be a nonstop marathon of public service whereby politicians who are tired or in need of a fresh perspective, as desired by their constituents, go back to their careers. Elected office is a calling where one's time comes and goes.

Deciding Whether to Run

Before jumping into my race, I asked of myself why I wanted to run. Was running more about doing something than trying to be someone? I believe in the principles that drew me into my race and have no doubt that they could deliver new and useful value for taxpayers of every income bracket. It was in the early stages of my candidacy when I was beginning to frame my campaign that I came across the "ambition theory of politics." Developed by Joseph Schlesinger, Professor

Emeritus of Political Science at Michigan State University, the theory offers three lenses through which the desire to enter politics can be viewed:

1. **Discrete Ambition:** A candidate driven by a cause enters the political fray for a finite amount of time before returning to the life he or she led before the election. In short, get elected, pursue and/or achieve your objective, and then return to being a regular citizen.

2. **Static Ambition:** This is where a politician remains in one office for an extended amount of time without expressing an interest to step down, pursue higher office, or move laterally. A politician in this category will perpetually run for reelection.

3. **Progressive Ambition:** A politician driven by this sort of ambition seeks election to increasingly powerful and prestigious offices, whether elected or appointed, in a climb up the political food chain.

Discrete ambition drew me into my race for Cook County Treasurer. I am not statically ambitious since I cannot seek reelection to an office that I do not currently hold. Finally, I am not progressively ambitious at this time. I entered my current race because an opportunity presented itself and the necessary stars aligned. Should

I be in elected office one day and the opportunity arise to serve in a position for which I am qualified and could positively impact issues dear to me, I'll have to decide then if I am progressively ambitious.

An interesting and objective way to inform the decision of whether to run is found in a formula published in the 1981 book, *Strategy and Choice in Congressional Elections*, by Gary C. Jacobson and Samuel Kernell, both professors of political science at the University of California in San Diego. The formula assigns a value to various factors a potential candidate should consider, and calculates whether the person should run:

$$U = P (Bw) + (1 - P) (BL) - C$$

U: utility of running for the office

P: probability of winning the election

Bw: candidate's perceived benefit of the office

BL: candidate's perceived benefit of the alternative they'll pursue if their race is unsuccessful

C: cost of running for the office, which includes the opportunity cost of vacating a currently held office and the net financial cost of the campaign.

If U is greater than zero and the benefits of alternative activities are not greater than U, the prospective candidate should run for office.

Although this formula does not quantify the quality of a candidate or their chances of winning an election, it provides a dispassionate way for a candidate to examine all possible angles before taking on the wildly fun sacrifice of running for office.

While I do think the formula's objective is pretty neat, please take the mention of that formula with a grain of salt. I did not utilize it when deciding to run, both because I did not know about it when I made my decision and because I doubt the formula's output would have overruled my conviction to pursue an office with the opportunity to create new value for the public. While I love the idea of using objective data to measure and make decisions, sometimes you have to trust your gut and knowingly defy what the numbers say. In the case of my current campaign, I feel so strongly about the unfulfilled potential in the office I am pursuing that no poll or solving for U was going to override my determination once my family was on board.

Engage with Grace and Civility

Running for office is scary and exhilarating and busy and hectic and wonderful. Candidates put more than their name on the ballot. They are putting their reputation on the line, along with everything they've built and become up to that point. If you're entertaining the idea of running, please know that a political campaign will only amplify and expose what's already inside of you.

Be sure that nothing you do or say during your campaign disagrees with the person you were before the race and the person you want to be the day after your win, lose, or withdraw.

A member of my campaign team, a seasoned Chicago political operative named Thom Karmik, once told me that "on this campaign, you'll have your best days and your worst days, sometimes on the same day, but you can't get too far up or too far down."

Karmik's advice reminded me of a favorite line from the 2001 movie *Blow*, in which, after filing for bankruptcy, Ray Liotta's character tells his young son "Sometimes you're flush and sometimes you're bust, and when you're up, it's never as good as it seems, and when you're down, you never think you'll be up again, but life goes on." On the campaign's best days and on its most trying days—and there continue to be plenty of both—I try to maintain focus and perspective by prioritizing my wife and daughter, which helps clear my mind and make everything else on my plate more manageable and enjoyable.

As the challenges and opportunities of a campaign change quickly and often without much notice, I try to mimic the stoic professional confidence demonstrated by my childhood hero, football legend Barry Sanders, whose talent and attitude transcended his circumstances and his sport.

Sanders is arguably the greatest running back to ever touch a football. Despite his unearthly talent and the extraordinary effort he exhibited during every game, and even though his team, the Detroit Lions, was typically on the short end of the final score, after every touchdown he scored, he reacted with the utmost humility. As eighty thousand spectators in The Pontiac Silverdome celebrated Sanders taking on and often beating the opponent's eleven defenders, he would calmly hand the ball to the official and act like it was just another day at the office. He took the same approach to winning the Heisman Trophy, setting college football's single season touchdown and rushing record, leading the Detroit Lions to the franchise's only playoff win since 1957, and scoring 109 touchdowns and rushing for 15,269 yards in 10 NFL seasons on rosters without another threatening offensive player.

Prior to playing against Sanders's Oklahoma State University team in 1987, then-University of Oklahoma Head Coach Barry Switzer instructed his team, "Whatever you do, don't hurt Thurman [Thomas]. You don't want to play against this freshman back they have named Barry Sanders."[†] Despite the accolades, the fear he invoked in his opponents, and the constant affirmation of his extraordinary ability, Sanders let his actions speak for him as he demonstrated humility at every level of the game. Whether he lost yards on a play or left an entire

---

†   Thurman Thomas was an All-American college football player and is currently enshrined in the NFL Hall of Fame alongside Barry Sanders.

defense in the dust on his way to the end zone, he never lost respect for himself or his opponent as he personified professionalism.

Sanders's character also shined off the field. Former Detroit Lions president Tom Lewand once recalled an instance before the 1997 NFL season when Sanders had signed the richest contract in league history at the time: six years for $36 million. Lewand had arrived at Saginaw Valley State University, the site of the team's training camp, just as Sanders was parking. Sanders asked Lewand to come over and see his new car—his reward to himself for signing the new deal. Lewand told what happened next:

> I go over, it's a black Jaguar, and I look in, I peek in the window, I go, "Barry, this car has 38,000 miles on it." He said, "I know, I got a great deal."

Sanders had the money to buy any car, especially a new one. With a sense of self that was not susceptible to the input of others or superficial achievements, and with an adherence to the undervalued virtues of modesty and humility, Sanders rose beyond superstar status and remains a relatable role model who positively influences my life.

Sanders abruptly retired from professional football in July 1999 with the same unceremonious approach he employed when calmly handing the ball to nearest referee after scoring a touchdown. No press conference, no tearful goodbye, no Q&A—just a faxed letter to his hometown newspaper, the *Wichita Eagle*. Whether he was running into the end zone or ending a Hall of Fame career, Sanders calmly and competently did his job with efficiency and class again and again and again.

Growing up as a fan of the Detroit Lions, many fall Sunday afternoons ended in heartbreak. But when they win the Super Bowl—and they will one day, is what I have to keep telling myself—even the sight of the franchise's longtime owners, the Ford family, accepting the Lombardi trophy on behalf of the generations of Lions fans, will not serve me as well as what I learned in my formative years by witnessing the multifaceted grace of Barry Sanders.

The Happy Warrior

During my days as an undergrad, I frequently wrote letters and requested meetings with the Fordham University president's office to ask questions or express my opinions on matters that were pressing to a twenty-year-old displeased with a feckless basketball team, objectively bad cafeteria food (rated the worst in the nation by *Princeton Review* as recently as 2012), plans for campus development, and a host of other issues that did not merit the time of the university president. However, university president Father Joseph McShane, SJ, generously humored me and, during one of those meetings, mentioned that the desk in his office had once belonged to the first

Catholic nominee for president, four-term governor of New York Alfred (Al) Smith.

The meeting during which Father McShane mentioned the desk occurred around the 2004 presidential election that resulted in President George W. Bush defeating Senator John Kerry of Massachusetts. Before that election (and before most presidential elections since 1945), the last event at which the candidates share a stage before one of them is elected as the next commander-in-chief is the Alfred E. Smith Memorial Foundation Dinner, better known as "The Al Smith Dinner." Held on the third Thursday of October before a presidential election, The Al Smith Dinner is an indispensable exhibition of sportsmanship and humor at the apex of a grueling national contest.

After learning about the desk and the dinner, my interest in Governor Smith was piqued.

The former New York governor's famous nickname, The Happy Warrior, was bestowed by Franklin Delano Roosevelt during the 1924 Democratic National Convention, when Smith was complimented as "the Happy Warrior of the political battlefield" for his infectious combination of enthusiasm and tenacity. Although Smith was unsuccessful in his 1928 campaign for the presidency, with the behavior of a gentleman and the production of a workhorse, he lit the spark for the social safety net from which the New Deal would grow and extended the belief that no one in America should be abandoned.

As president, FDR would go on to say, "Practically all the things we've done in the federal government are the things Al Smith did as governor of New York."

The image of the Happy Warrior personified by Al Smith is in the back of my mind, at the bottom of my heart, and on the tip of my tongue every time I part from my wife and daughter to attend a campaign-related event, every time I call a friend or family member to ask for financial support, every time I try to give my stump speech with more enthusiasm and optimism than the countless other times I've recited it, or every time I meet someone who is personally concerned about the office I am seeking and how my platform could affect them or someone they love.

Running for office, going to work day in and day out, patiently and attentively parenting, being present in a conversation you may not want to have, eating right, exercising, reading books and newspapers rather than just social media posts—it requires a lot of work, and sacrificing time, for recreation, relaxation, and with loved ones. However, with a smile and a positive response when asked why I'm running or even just how I'm doing, I remind myself of the unique opportunity to run for public office. In fact, my campaign manager, Sean Tenner, a cheery and brilliant Chicagoan known for his work ethic and knack for constructing innovative campaigns, regularly emphasizes the importance of the Happy Warrior approach not just for the effect it has on voters, elected officials, and political observers, but also on the candidate, too.

Rivalries can be fun and competition is healthy, but hatred is never productive. Hating your opposition is a direct line to distraction, not to victory or lasting satisfaction. No matter your personal opinion of your opponent, it's important to embrace the Happy Warrior identity by staying above the small-minded pettiness that tells voters that you are no better than a stereotypical politician. Running for office, along with starting a business or raising a family, is all too time-consuming, too expensive, and too much work if you are not any having fun, so at the very least, enjoy the privilege of your experiences as you pursue your goal.

Respect and Empathy

Empathy is perhaps the most practical and valuable of all human traits, and it is indispensable in effective public service. As Doris Kearns Goodwin wrote in *Team of Rivals: The Political Genius of Abraham Lincoln*, "[Lincoln] possessed extraordinary empathy—the gift or curse of putting himself in the place of another, to experience what they were feeling, to understand their motives and desires." Empathy is the root of The Golden Rule (*i.e.*, do unto others what you would have done unto you), and it is the most direct route to building healthy relationships. Politics is an amplified microcosm of humanity in which our best and worst traits are in close quarters under a microscope, thus I would argue that empathy is the most important of any political resource.

President Truman once said, "Democrats work to help people who need help. That other party, they work for people who don't need help. That's all there is to it." However entertaining and effective President Truman's words might be for reaching people who are already of a left-leaning point of view, that approach won't help attract those people who would be made to feel like they are selling out or admitting guilt for past votes by crossing party lines. A productive strategy for growing the Democratic party must be more than we are right and good and they are evil and selfish. Constructive criticism should strive to target differences in policy, rather than stoop to overly personal attacks.

In his May 2017 address to Class Day at Yale University, Vice President Joe Biden spoke of an unforgettable lesson from his first term as a U.S. Senator when he learned to limit his questioning to a person's judgment and to keep an individual's motivation off limits from criticism since one never fully knows what makes another person tick. At the time, Biden had taken issue with criticism from Senator Jesse Helms of North Carolina regarding a bill for disabled citizens. Biden felt like a fool when he was told by Senator Mike Mansfield of Montana that Helms had a disabled child, which influenced his position on the bill. Mansfield permanently enlightened Biden when he advised him to adopt the policy of questioning judgement but never motivation. As Biden told the audience at Yale, "When you question a man's motives, when you say they're acting out of greed or in the pocket of an interest group, it's awful hard to reach consensus."

You can work with someone after saying that you disagree with their vote or stance because it is not in the interest of those you serve. You can work with someone after disagreeing with them on impersonal and objective grounds. But to say that someone acted a certain way because they are dimwitted or heartless— i.e., to launch an *ad hominem* attack—will fracture any hope for a productive and respectful relationship and lead to partisan gridlock and vitriol that in no way benefits the public.

Commit to Your Priorities and Let's Go

When undertaking a monumental task, your efforts cannot be fueled by a desire to satisfy anyone more than yourself. The long nights and lonely hours of grinding must mean the most to you. Someone else's validation, no matter how desired, will never capture the extent of what you've personally given to chase down your goal.

As U.S. Attorney General, Robert Kennedy was building a case against the head of the Teamsters Union, Jimmy Hoffa. Richard North Patterson has recounted an occasion during Kennedy's pursuit when he was heading home around two in the morning after working on the

Hoffa case and drove past Hoffa's office to see that the lights were still on. Refusing to risk being outworked, Kennedy turned around and headed back to his office at the Justice Department. Some people are more gifted than others and some people have more powerful networks, but hard work, which costs nothing, is priceless and nontransferable. A person can have talent, brains, money, and charisma, but if they are not willing to outwork the competition, then all of those advantages are at increased risk of not being enough. A strong work ethic can take mediocre people far, and the absence of a willingness to work is usually why those with potential never get as far as they could have.

Once you make progress or finally arrive at your destination, never forget that you have the capability to dig deeper to another level of drive and persistence. Get knocked down, it doesn't matter. You are The Terminator, or some other unstoppable force in human form, standing back up and wasting no time on humiliation or self-doubt, looking straight ahead, and continuing on your path, undeterred.

People will presume that you cannot win, even those with whom you are socially or professionally aligned. Learn from them, do not obey them, and move forward. Digest their perspective and consider it a peek inside your opposition. Get hit with a negative comment under the guise of expertise—it does not matter. Fail and critics will smugly say from the safety of the sidelines that they told you so; win and they'll just shrug their shoulders since they were never invested enough to be affected by the outcome. Belief in yourself and your rationale is all that matters. Your victory will always be far sweeter than the satisfaction of proving wrong someone who never knew you well enough to know that you were capable of not being denied your objective.

If you are fortunate enough to run for office, please enjoy it. You are participating in a part of our democracy that affects everyone but few ever experience. I don't know if I will win my current race, but this process is honestly the most fun I've ever had, and I am grateful for every day on the campaign trail. The happy warrior example set by Al Smith gives me guidance and context on the tough days and an even bigger reason to smile on the good ones.

∿

To those who think the Millennial generation is a collection of lazy, entitled, late bloomers reluctant to leave their parents' basement, know that we are coming. We are driven, we are smart, and we will do what no generation has done before because no other generation to this point has had access to greater opportunity.

To other members of the Millennial generation, we must consistently demand more of ourselves if we want to achieve a lasting and significant legacy in our finite stretch of time.

"First they ignore you. Then they ridicule you. And they attack you and want to burn you. And then they build monuments to you." That was said by Nicholas Klein in a May 15, 1918, address to the Amalgamated Clothing Workers of America. The Millennial generation is currently at risk of being "burned" in another way, by missing its opportunity to shape the institutions that impact our world. We should be concerned about the years ahead when we've fully inherited the mantle of leadership. By that time, we could very well spend many of our most productive years addressing matters that would not have been as consuming had we engaged earlier (i.e., now). Our opportunity, our arrival into leadership positions, must be earned through campaigns and candidates rooted in progressive and just principles. We can begin to repair the negative feelings associated with the word "politician" through policies that benefit the forgotten and underserved among us.

To our predecessors who cling to leadership positions out of a prevailing commitment to personal pride over the public good, you have our respect, but you do not have our deference or our patience.

To the giants, if you are fit to lead, then you are fit to compete, and for everyone's sake, may the best person win. My generation and I welcome the challenge to outwork, outmaneuver, and outlast anyone who prefers that we wait our turn from the sidelines.

Now is the time to lead. Now is the time to join or start a local civic organization. Now is the time to run for office. Now is the time to set the expectations and best practices that will raise the bar for all generations to come. Now is the time for our generation to step up and fully arrive.

Index

Acknowledgments

This book would not have been undertaken without the support and inspiration drawn from a number of individuals who have impacted my life. While I'll never be able to thank every person whose relationship or message has helped me along, and I sincerely apologize to anyone whose name I have unintentionally omitted, below are some of those whose special contributions must be acknowledged.

First, thank you to my immediate family: my wife, Karishma, and daughter, Reshma; my parents, Robert and Katy Gariepy, and Karishma's parents, Rajesh and Arti Vora; Emily, Chris and Kate Janus; Roma Vora; Anne and Jimmy Amine.

Thanks too to our wonderful extended family: Rosemary and Louis Gariepy; Betty and John Yuhas; Manhar and Chandrakant Vora; Rasila and Vinod Shah;

Don and Carol Roble; Julie and Byron Flint; Amy and Nick Rouech; Susie and Christoph Söhnchen; Lindsay and Adam Lawrie; Carrie Roble; Suzie and Ron Ludgin; Beth and Brian Henry; Brian Henry; Molly Henry; Kevin Henry; Suanne and Lloyd Lassiter; Elizabeth Lassiter and Mike Schubert; Lyle Lassiter; Bill Brown; Ellen Brown and Howard Schwager; Lillie and Austin Brown; Allison Brown; Roopa and Rahul Parikh; Natasha Parikh; Anita Parikh; Shaan Parikh; Hetal Shah and Kartik Ganeshan; Rohan Ganeshan; Shivani Ganeshan; Ajay and Rekha Vora; Shephali and Benedikt Graf; and Satyen and Sarah Vora.

My appreciation to our neighbors, especially Marcia Wachowiak, and The East Village Association.

Special thanks to our friends, including Jimmy Coggan; Ashley Shah; Sonia Shah; Payal Shah; Bansi and Akash Bhalla; Vaishali Patel; Shreena and Daniel Fulani; Meera Shah; Poonam and Ameet Mahale; Nirali and Justin Lee; Neil Shah; Akta and Mike Bradshaw; Gina and Avery Hagedorn; Bryan and Michelle Dow; Carolyn Kassnoff; Kathleen and Chris Vamos; Mia Starks; Chris Hintermeister; Jennifer and Jordan Pasternak; Irwin Reiter; Melissa Piorkowski and Adam Tymowski; Lindsay and Mike Rademacher; Brian Beglin; Sarah and Shawn McGurn; Meghan and Paul Hammond; Hilary and Kyle Hanson; Kristin and Adam Widlak; Stephanie and Greg Maczka; Rebecca and Jeff Tatom; Emily and John Wilson;

Katie and Tyler Kiefner; Christina Bergeron and Kyle Pine; Kelly and Dustin Harrington.

I'm grateful for the guidance and friendship of those I've met on my journey in politics, including J.R. Patton; Nick Daggers; Sean Tenner and Shiwali Varshney; Thom Karmik; Greg Bales; Ed Gray; Tim Nazanin; Marc Lane, Tim Brandhorst, and Mandy Lane; Shefali Razdan Duggal; Dan Johnson; and Raja Krishnamoorthi.

My former colleagues at Amtrak continue to inspire me: Ray Lang; Jonathan Hutchison; Alex Khalfin; Rob Eaton; Joe McHugh; Robert Glass; Derrick James; Paul Sanders; Charlie Monte Verde; Mike Franke; Dorothy Bailey; Dick Rogers; Vernae Graham; Jeff White; Suzanne Fike; Meredith Benton; Robin McCarthy; and Patrick Merrill.

I'm grateful to my friends, teachers, and mentors at U of D Jesuit, including David "Bernie" Nichols; Lauren and Francesco Iacobelli; Jeff Shelton; Ross Oermann; Eric Oermann; Marilyn Oermann; Dave Oermann; Drew DeFour; Richard Siemion; Vinny Abatemarco; Rick Bennetts; Paul Diehl; Jim Boynton; SJ. Derrick Lopez; Karl Kiser; SJ. Jim Moran; Lynne Rinke; Dan Hill; Mary Lakamp; Chuck Gumbel; Tom Coyne; Ron Torina, SJ; to those at Fordham, including Mike Tueth, SJ; Aaron Kirchner; J-Glenn Murray, SJ; Christopher Capuzzi; Michael Klett; Dan Griffin; Dan Jenney; John Siracuse; Malorie McLaughlin; Vicki Hertlein-Perez; Rosa Romeo; Barbara Porco; Peter Olinto; Joseph McShane, SJ; and to those at Northwestern, including Joseph Schofer; Aaron Gellman; Diana Marek; Marco Nie; Pablo Durango-Cohen; Christopher Lindsey; and Charlotte and Andi Frei.

Finally, I'm indebted to all those whom I've mentioned by name in the book, particularly Louis J. Gariepy; Michelle and Barack Obama; Joe Biden; Ruth Bader Ginsburg; Harold Washington; Thomas Jefferson; Aaron Sorkin; James Madison; Zachary Fardon; John F. Kennedy; Shel Silverstein; David Orr; Martin Luther King, Jr.; Mike Quigley; David Axelrod; George Washington; Cincinnatus; Abraham Lincoln; Warren Buffett; Al Smith; and Barry Sanders.

About the Author

Peter Gariepy is a candidate for the Democratic nomination for Cook County Treasurer. He and his wife, Karishma, live in Chicago with their daughter, Reshma, and their rescue dog, Baloney.

He was graduated from The University of Detroit Jesuit High School and Academy, received a Bachelors in Public Accounting and a Masters in Taxation from Fordham University, and a Masters in Civil Engineering from Northwestern University. He is a licensed Certified Public Accountant in the State of Illinois.

Peter has written two children's books, *Harold's Home Station* and *The Tooth Fairy Has No Off-Season*.

81740290R00099

Made in the USA
Lexington, KY
21 February 2018

GRASS

ITS PRODUCTION AND

UTILIZATION

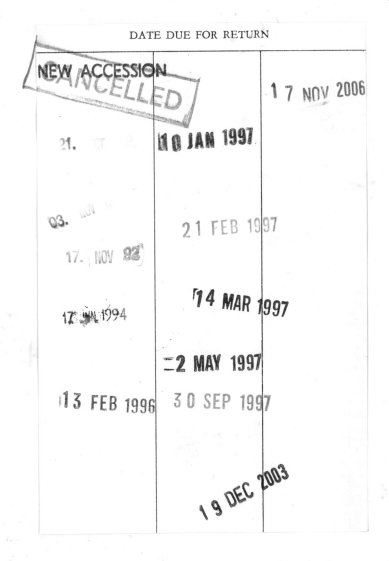